"If you or someone you know is suffering from the ag[...]sive compulsive disorder (OCD), read this book! You'll learn that you are not alone—and you'll learn about a proven and effective treatment for OCD: exposure and response prevention (ERP). Joan Davidson explains in clear and accessible language, with plenty of practical exercises, what to expect and how to prepare for treatment. What makes this book truly unique is that Davidson includes the stories of three very different people who regained control over their lives through this treatment. Their stories are authentic, inspiring, and full of hope. This straightforward and compassionate approach to ERP is a real contribution for clients—and for clinicians, this text is an invaluable resource for improving our skills at helping clients commit to treatment."

> —**Laura B. Mason, PhD,** clinical professor in the department of
> psychology at University of California, Berkeley and associate
> director of the UC Berkeley psychology clinic

"Exposure and response prevention is the most effective treatment technique for OCD. Davidson makes these scientifically proven strategies very accessible in this excellent book. Working through it on your own, or with the help of a professional, should reduce obsessions and compulsions."

> —**Jonathan S. Abramowitz, PhD,** professor and associate chair of
> psychology at the University of North Carolina at Chapel Hill

"Practical and matter-of-fact, yet simultaneously deep and compassionate, *Daring to Challenge OCD* is made-to-order for anyone plagued by obsessions and compulsions, including family members and loved ones. Loaded with wisdom, science, and clear case examples, it authoritatively documents what OCD is and how to treat it. To my mind, this is *the* go-to book on the topic across the entire field. Run, don't walk, to get this book and read it!"

> —**Stephen P. Hinshaw, PhD,** professor of psychology at the University
> of California, Berkeley, and vice-chair of psychology in the
> department of psychiatry at University of California, San Francisco

"Davidson, with the help of her brave and articulate clients, illuminates a healing path for those suffering from OCD and the therapists who want to help them. I recommend this book to anyone who struggles with the problem or who cares about someone who does."

—**Mary Pipher, PhD,** author of *Reviving Ophelia* and
The Green Boat

"A fantastic book about obsessive compulsive disorder (OCD) and its gold standard treatment! This book provides answers to anyone struggling to understand OCD and offers a blueprint for what to expect in treatment. It describes the experiences of three individuals—each with a different kind of OCD—and provides hope and motivation for positive change. I wish it had been in print when I was first diagnosed."

—**Paula Kotakis,** San Francisco OCD support group facilitator

"Three individuals with obsessive compulsive disorder (OCD), guided by the author, a talented therapist, tell the stories of their illness and their treatment in blow-by-blow detail. Any person who suffers from OCD, loves someone who suffers from OCD, or treats OCD, should read this book."

—**Jacqueline B. Persons, PhD,** director of the Cognitive Behavior
Therapy and Science Center and clinical professor in the
department of psychology at the University of California, Berkeley

"*Daring to Challenge OCD* is a long overdue, step-by-step treatment manual that offers hope to those struggling to tackle the complexities inherent in exposure and response prevention therapy. Offering personal, firsthand accounts of what it's like to go through the treatment process, this easy-to-read, wonderfully well-written tool is a must-have for those needing to guide their own treatment and who may not otherwise have access to expert therapists. The compassionate approach in this book will help many overcome their fear of treatment and embrace their new journey toward recovery of their OCD."

—**Robin Zasio, PsyD, LCSW,** president of the International
OCD Foundation, featured doctor on A&E's *Hoarders,* and
author of *The Hoarder in You*

DARING TO CHALLENGE OCD

Overcome Your Fear of Treatment
& Take Control of Your Life Using
Exposure & Response Prevention

JOAN DAVIDSON, PhD

New Harbinger Publications, Inc.

Publisher's Note

Distributed in Canada by Raincoast Books

Copyright © 2014 by Joan Davidson
New Harbinger Publications, Inc.
5674 Shattuck Avenue
Oakland, CA 94609
http://www.newharbinger.com

Cover design by Amy Shoup
Acquired by Catharine Meyers
Edited by Jasmine Star

Library of Congress Cataloging-in-Publication Data

Davidson, Joan, 1960-
 Daring to challenge OCD : overcome your fear of treatment and take control of your life using exposure and response prevention / Joan Davidson, PhD.
     pages cm
  Includes bibliographical references.
  ISBN 978-1-60882-859-3 (paperback) -- ISBN 978-1-60882-860-9 (pdf e-book) -- ISBN 978-1-60882-861-6 (epub) 1. Obsessive-compulsive disorder--Treatment. 2. Exposure therapy. I. Title. II. Title: Daring to challenge obsessive-compulsive disorder.
  RC533.D35 2014
  616.85'227--dc23

                    2014006467

Printed in the United States of America

16   15   14

10   9   8   7   6   5   4   3   2   1   First printing

To Miriam and Jack

CONTENTS

ACKNOWLEDGMENTS

Many people deserve acknowledgment for their roles in making this book possible. I am tremendously grateful to the three people who allowed me to share their personal stories to help demystify OCD and bring treatment to life. In addition to daring to challenge OCD, they dared to share their struggles and triumphs so that others could learn from their stories. They worked with fabulous therapists, whom I must also thank not only for supporting this project but also for providing first-rate treatment, allowing all of us to benefit from their clients' successes.

I thank Mary Samson for sharing her story and offering unwavering enthusiasm, wit, and wisdom. Her encouragement continually reminded me why this book is so worthwhile. I thank her therapist, Chad LeJeune, for his support of this project and consultation regarding how he integrates acceptance and commitment therapy and exposure and response prevention in treating OCD. I thank Gina for her tireless commitment to this book and for courageously sharing her story about living with and seeking treatment to cope with terrifying thoughts and unrelenting doubts. Gina chose not to disclose her full name due to possible consequences if her OCD symptoms were misinterpreted by people in her community, reflecting how important it is that she shared her story in an effort to help others develop a better understanding of OCD. I thank Ted Herzberg for sharing his long-term struggles with OCD and honest appraisals about treatment, and for offering ongoing support and insights about the utility of this book. In my practice, I've been fortunate to work with many clients whose courage in challenging OCD makes my job so rewarding. Their observations, creativity, and golden nuggets of wisdom aid and encourage my work and are reflected in the pages of this book.

I extend a huge thank-you to my editor, Angela Autry Gorden, for her steadfast patience, guidance, and advice, and to Jasmine Star, who meticulously helped me refine this manuscript and whose enthusiasm and thoughtfulness bolstered my spirits during the process. Thank you to Matt McKay and Catharine Meyers for supporting this project through its many permutations and to Jess Beebe and Nicola Skidmore for their contributions to its development. I appreciate New Harbinger's passion and dedication to publishing works that can improve peoples' lives, and I'm grateful for the warm welcome and opportunity to contribute to that mission.

I particularly want to thank Jacqueline B. Persons, a mentor, colleague, and friend who has guided and supported me at every step in my professional career, including writing this book. I also thank my colleagues at the San Francisco Bay Area Center for Cognitive Therapy—Daniela Owen, Michael Tompkins, and Daniel Weiner—and colleagues Rochelle Frank, Janie Hong, and Polina Eidelman for their ongoing support and encouragement. In addition, I'm especially grateful to Patricia Zurita Ona and Kimberly Wilson not only for sharing their enthusiasm for this project but for reviewing the manuscript and offering sound advice and suggestions at various stages of its development. I also thank Stephen Hinshaw, Daniel Taube, and John Fleer for their guidance and encouragement as I developed the idea for this book. And while there are too many clinicians and researchers in the field to mention them by name, it's through their dedicated work that I've gained invaluable insights into treatment for OCD.

I especially want to thank Raja Tannous for his endless support, love, and patience as I take time away from our life together to work on projects, including this book, that are so meaningful to me. Thank you to Nadya and Lilliana Tannous for their constant encouragement, and to the many Tannous, Pierce, and Davidson family members, as well as Lorraine and Carl Fries, for cheering on this book project. I offer a special note of love and appreciation to the memories of John Davidson, David Wusterbarth, Shirley Johnson, and Ronald Bushman, who excitedly followed the progress of this book as long as was possible.

FOREWORD

What if? Ask most anyone with OCD to share a recent obsession, and chances are it will begin with those two words. *What if this doorknob is contaminated? What if I accidentally ran someone over?* The variations are endless—as are the nonsensical rituals, or compulsions, that these disturbing questions spawn. As someone who spent the better part of a decade debilitated by this disorder, I know "What if...?" questions all too well, and I also know the importance of learning to sit with the discomfort they present. This book provides a wonderful overview of how that's done. But what sets it apart from so many other books about OCD is that it also addresses another set of questions that people with OCD face when entering treatment. I've come to think of these as healthy, "How can...?" questions about the process itself, such as *How can I stay motivated to do the hard work of OCD therapy?*

I've found that recovering from the worst of OCD requires learning to navigate both types of questions, and Joan Davidson has done a masterful job of providing guidance regarding each. Moreover, by weaving in the observations of three people with OCD, she also offers readers powerful insights not often available outside of support groups.

The good news about OCD treatment is that it works. I say this as someone who has experienced firsthand the benefits of the proven strategies Joan details in these pages, and also as someone who, through years of OCD outreach, has witnessed scores of almost unfathomable recoveries. Cognitive behavioral therapy and, more specifically, exposure and response prevention (ERP) can rescue people from the grips of OCD. I've seen it happen again and again. But here's the catch: this treatment is challenging—very challenging. In essence, ERP requires that people sit with their anxiety regarding their very worst fears, those "What if...?" questions that create discomfort beyond what most people without OCD can even comprehend. By not sugarcoating the reality of the challenges of treatment, Joan does her readers a great service. And by offering guidance on motivation, she goes one very important step further.

In the quest to stay motivated, harnessing the power of healthy questions can make all the difference. As readers will learn in this book, strategies from acceptance and commitment therapy (ACT) can help anyone in treatment ask empowering questions, such as *How can I see the big picture here?* and *How can I stay fully engaged in the process?* For me, it's all about identifying and pursuing what I've come to call "greater good" goals, and Joan includes a full chapter on this general concept, addressing why treatment is worth it. In a similar fashion, she and the three people with OCD who have contributed to this book anticipate and answer question after question that anyone newly diagnosed with OCD will probably have, and *should* have, about the treatment process.

Whether you are someone with OCD, a family member, or a seasoned treatment provider, the information in these pages has much to offer you. I am certain—not a word that we with OCD use lightly!—that this book is going to help a lot of people.

—Jeff Bell
Author, *Rewind, Replay, Repeat:*
A Memoir of Obsessive-Compulsive Disorder

INTRODUCTION

When new clients come to my office, they have frightening images and thoughts regarding treatment. They wonder, *What kinds of things will my therapist expect me to do? Will treatment be too difficult for me to handle? Will I be asked to do things that put me at risk?* New clients want to know the nuts and bolts of treatment. They want to know what treatment actually looks like.

Perhaps you've read that cognitive behavioral therapy offers effective treatment for obsessive-compulsive disorder (OCD). You may already be familiar with the term "exposure and response prevention" (ERP), which is the gold standard of treatment for OCD. It involves intentionally facing obsessions and tolerating the anxiety and discomfort they provoke without using compulsions. When you have OCD, this may be the last thing you want to do! ERP can sound scary. However, the chances are quite good that this treatment can help you.

You may feel caught between a rock and a hard place. You want to rid yourself of OCD symptoms and free yourself from spending so much time and energy battling with frightening thoughts and images. You want to break away from the burden of managing daily encounters with anything that triggers anxiety and the endless cycles of seeking certainty and reassurance. Yet what you've heard about ERP probably sounds like a hard pill to swallow. As awful as OCD is, therapy that involves facing your worst fears may also sound awful. So in addition to feeling stressed by your symptoms, now you may feel stressed by deciding whether to begin a treatment that sounds even more stressful. Making the decision to start treatment takes a lot of courage.

Why I Wrote This Book

I wrote this book to help people with OCD move forward from this quandary. This is a practical, go-to book that answers questions I commonly hear in my practice—questions like these:

- *How did my behaviors become such a big problem?*

- *Do people like me get better?*

- *How will therapy help me change my behaviors?*

- *I have really bad thoughts that I'm afraid to say out loud; does that mean something terrible about me?*

- *How will therapy help me deal with bad thoughts?*

- *ERP sounds really hard and scary. Why should I do it?*

- *Is there an easier way to overcome OCD?*

- *Won't OCD just pop up in some other way?*

- *Will treatment be worth it?*

You'll find answers to these questions and more in this book. I hope these answers will help you embark on treatment that can free you from so much suffering.

Whether you're apprehensive about starting treatment, nervous as you begin treatment, discouraged because you've encountered obstacles during treatment, or seeking practical tips and advice as you complete treatment, this book will take you through the nitty-gritty practicalities of all phases of treatment for OCD using ERP. I describe OCD, its underlying themes, and how people get stuck in an OCD cycle. I guide you through what treatment is like from beginning to end and show you how treatment for OCD differs slightly depending on the nature of the obsessions and compulsions, the willingness of the client, and the therapist's style. ERP isn't as cookie-cutter as you may think.

I describe what I typically see and hear in my clinical practical, and I offer suggestions, just as I do with clients in my office. I hope to inform you, clarify any misconceptions, and encourage you to pursue and complete treatment. This is the book I've wanted to offer my clients. It's not a self-help treatment protocol, but rather a guide to help you understand your symptoms, consider why treatment is worth it, get a glimpse into real-life treatments, and overcome obstacles that you may encounter in treatment.

Benefiting from Others' Experience

In this book you'll hear from others who have been in treatment for OCD. Their stories can be especially helpful if you're afraid to begin treatment or are having trouble sticking with it. In OCD support groups, veteran group members offer inspiration by educating and encouraging new members. They give hope to newcomers, who often fear treatment as much as they fear OCD triggers. When you hit inevitable bumps along the road to recovery, the experience of seasoned clients can provide helpful guidance. Because you might not have access to support groups or to others who have completed treatment for OCD, this book provides accounts of three people with OCD who have been successfully treated. It was important to me to include real-life stories of people with different types of OCD who have been there and can share their unique perspectives on OCD and treatment. I weave their stories throughout the book to guide you in your journey. I hope you find their stories informative and their courage and resourcefulness when daring to challenge OCD inspiring.

To find the people whose stories I've included, I contacted local cognitive behavioral therapists with expertise in treating OCD and asked them to spread the word to current and former clients that I wanted to write about real stories of OCD treatment. Three clients with very different OCD symptoms—Mary, Gina, and Ted—contacted me and shared their experiences. Their stories are real, and each of them offers their personal experiences and insights in the hope of helping others.

Mary

Mary is an account director with a background in advertising, and also works as an actor and playwright. She struggles with a form of OCD related to feelings of contamination that led to attempts to suppress or analyze disturbing thoughts and images and engage in compulsive behaviors of washing, cleaning, and researching for reassurance. Mary's fears and compulsions eventually permeated all aspects of her life, including friendships, relationships, and work. Her treatment highlights ERP, the essential component of OCD treatment, with strategies to practice "leaning in" toward disturbing thoughts and images. Her therapist uses components from a type of cognitive behavioral therapy called acceptance and commitment therapy to help her understand the rationale for leaning in and build the courage to willingly face her fears without using compulsions. Mary often uses creative imagery to practice exposure to feared images, and as a playwright and performer, she shares her struggles with and triumphs over OCD onstage.

Gina

Gina recently graduated from college and has begun a new career. She and her husband have four children and are actively involved in their church. She suffers from a type of OCD that involves aggressive and sexual obsessions, which led to internal torment, reassurance seeking, and avoidance. Gina was preoccupied by fears that having violent thoughts meant she could be capable of acting on them. Her doubt spread to unrelenting questions about her sexual orientation. Although therapists who specialize in treating OCD commonly see clients with these kinds of fears and doubts, people troubled by these thoughts are often terrified to tell anyone about them and suffer silently instead. Gina bravely discusses her intrusive thoughts and fears to help others know that they are not alone. Her treatment, using ERP, illustrates what it takes to face terrifying obsessive thoughts like *How do I know that I won't drown my baby?* She also shares her struggle to find the courage to face her fears instead of trying to avoid having them.

Ted

Ted is a former Franciscan priest. After leaving the priesthood, he worked for twenty-five years as an investigator of discrimination for the state of California. In recent years, Ted has enjoyed retirement by volunteering as a mentor at an elementary school, pursuing writing projects and an online business, and spending time with his family. Ted's OCD symptoms involve concerns about morality and beliefs that he could potentially be responsible for harm coming to others. For decades, he agonized about doing things "just right" and suffered due to doubting his actions. He engaged in unrelenting self-questioning, reassurance seeking, and checking behaviors. When he left the priesthood, doubts and fears about making mistakes tormented him in new ways. He determinedly sought help, but because OCD wasn't well understood, his symptoms went undiagnosed for decades. Recently, thanks to the proliferation of research and accessibility of information about OCD, Ted enthusiastically pursued treatment using ERP. He discusses his initial treatment success and optimism, along with his ongoing struggle to not use compulsions when facing unpredictable intrusions of doubts about past and recent actions.

Other Case Examples

Throughout the book I use other people to illustrate different types of OCD and various components of treatment. The cases I describe reflect my experiences treating clients with OCD, but are not based on particular clients' stories or treatment. Since OCD symptoms are diverse, the examples and stories in this book vary quite a bit. I encourage you to read them all. Even if stories about particular symptoms and treatment examples don't directly target your type of OCD, the underlying themes will be similar. Therefore, you can learn a lot from the range of examples throughout the book.

Working with This Book

You'll need to have a notebook or journal on hand to complete many of the exercises and write down your answers to questions I pose throughout the book. These exercises and questions are designed to help you understand your symptoms, resolve hesitation about committing to treatment, plan for treatment, and come up with solutions to overcome obstacles that you might encounter. I also hope you'll take notes and write questions so you can bring them with you to discuss with a therapist.

I know how scary it can be to learn about treatment for OCD. I know that ERP isn't always easy to embrace. There's no quick and effortless fix. Effective treatment requires a commitment to immersing yourself in practicing new responses to your fears. From my clinical experience, I also know how rewarding it is for people to take the plunge and successfully reclaim their lives from the grips of OCD. Even though treatment may sound scary or difficult, I encourage you to commit to it. The rewards for learning to face your fears rather than avoiding them can be great. Most importantly, you can live the life you want to live—a life not limited by obsessions and compulsions.

CHAPTER 1

UNDERSTANDING OCD

It can be hard to commit to treatment if you don't understand your problem. Although you may already know you have symptoms of OCD, you might have many questions. You might wonder how your thoughts and behaviors became so problematic when they somehow make good sense. Washing and cleaning are good hygiene practices. Checking to be certain that you don't make mistakes seems reasonable. Counting to "lucky" numbers or arranging items "just right" may seem harmless. You might feel anxious because you have frightening intrusive thoughts and wonder why anyone wouldn't try to make them go away. People have such idiosyncratic variations of OCD that they sometimes fear their symptoms are too unique for treatment to work for them. Understanding OCD will help you understand your symptoms and how treatment works, no matter how unique your thoughts and behaviors may seem.

Although there is greater access to information about OCD than ever before, misconceptions still flourish. Popular culture seems to have adopted "OCD" as a term to describe ordinary desires for cleanliness and orderliness. It isn't uncommon to hear someone joke, "Oh, that's just my OCD!" It may not be easy to hear something you struggle with being laughed at and casually minimized as a problem that everyone experiences. Fictional characters with OCD are portrayed in movies and television programs, but how they are portrayed may not accurately reflect the suffering and challenges you face. You may fear that something is wrong with you because you have thoughts that seem much more disturbing than what you see in the media. You might wonder if your thoughts are so specific to you that others can't understand what you endure.

OCD can seem confusing because the outward symptoms look so diverse. What do you picture when you think about OCD? Do you picture someone frequently washing her hands? Do you picture someone repeatedly checking door locks? Do you picture someone lining up objects until they're "just right"? Many images may come to mind. The range of compulsive behaviors is wide. It's important to understand the nature of obsessions and compulsions so that treatment makes good sense to you. Even though symptoms are different, similar underlying mechanisms, or themes, are in play. Understanding your symptoms will lay the groundwork for understanding how exposure and response prevention (ERP) works.

What Are Obsessions?

These days, people often say things like, "Oh, I'm just obsessing about such and such," meaning they keep thinking about something or talking about it, but usually they aren't feeling especially distressed. However, true obsessions are very distressing. *Obsessions* are "recurrent and persistent thoughts, urges, or images that are experienced as intrusive and unwanted" (American Psychiatric Association 2013). They aren't intentional. They include thoughts like *What if I contaminate my family because I stepped on something dirty? What if I accidentally hit a pedestrian while driving to work? What if something bad happens to someone I love because I didn't repeat lucky numbers in my head? What if I lose control and stab my husband?* When you have OCD, you wish that thoughts like these would stop popping into your head. Obsessive thoughts intrude frequently and with great intensity. It feels impossible to stop them, and they cause substantial anxiety or distress.

The content of obsessions isn't different from the types of thoughts most people might have. People who don't have OCD experience disturbing thoughts, but they can usually dismiss them and let them go.

When you have OCD, however, certain thoughts have a way of sticking. Mary described OCD thoughts as "sticking like Velcro," and this imagery rings true for my clients. Some thoughts or images feel like they stick and seem especially important. They keep returning and are often very intense. Mary joked about needing Drano to clear obsessions that got stuck in her head, then said, "If you have OCD, I don't have to tell you how awful it is to have something that you can't get out of your mind. If you don't have OCD, imagine having to watch something disturbing on television over and over again, unable to turn it off. You don't want this to keep popping up in your mind!"

Many types of thoughts can "stick like Velcro" and cause great distress for people with OCD. This is one reason why OCD can seem so confusing. While one person has obsessions about germs and contamination, another has obsessions about being capable of harming loved ones. The content of obsessions usually falls into general categories, and you may have obsessions from more than one category. You can also have obsessions that don't neatly fit into categories. In addition, the content of obsessions can shift over time. You may struggle with one type of obsession and later discover that you also struggle with another type.

Contamination

Most people want to avoid germs and contaminants. Where individuals fit on the continuum of hygienic practices and desire for cleanliness varies. Our culture emphasizes cleanliness and protection from germs. We see it in advertisements for cleaning products, grocery stores entrances with antibacterial wipes, and public restrooms designed so occupants never have to touch a fixture. Contamination obsessions usually focus on germs, diseases, bodily fluids, and potential health hazards such as toxic cleaning supplies or pest-control products. If you have this type of OCD, you experience excessively high levels of anxiety or disgust when exposed to triggers of contamination obsessions and probably become preoccupied with avoiding them. In addition to fearing being exposed to contaminants yourself, you may also fear being responsible for contaminating others. For example, thoughts about contamination might go something like this: *If I touched something and became contaminated, items in my house that I touch will be contaminated. My family might touch them and become contaminated. If other people touch anything that I've touched, I'll be responsible for contaminating them too!*

If you have this type of OCD, you may believe that you can't handle how uncomfortable you'll feel if you come into contact with things that look or feel disgusting. Exposure to indistinguishable substances that are brown or red may trigger strong anxiety or disgust responses due to concerns of possibly coming into contact with bodily wastes and blood. It may be difficult to encounter substances that feel sticky, including gum and certain foods, lotions, and hair products. Yet if you have small children, it's especially difficult to avoid contact with bodily fluids or sticky substances all day long!

Emotional contamination is an OCD subtype involving fear of contact with certain people, items, or places because they feel dangerous or contaminated due to negative associations. For example, the clothes you wore when seeing something unclean, indistinguishable, or unpleasant can feel contaminated by association. If you have an unwanted sexual thought while walking in front of a certain store, the store may then feel contaminated. You may view people as contaminated due to their association with someone or something you deem to be undesirable or dangerous.

Many of Mary's obsessions involved preoccupations with indistinguishable objects and feeling disturbed by not knowing exactly what she had seen. When she saw people who somehow looked strange to her but she couldn't tell what was "wrong" with them, she felt contaminated by having seen them. This made her want to shower and discard the clothes and shoes she was wearing and any items she had on her when she saw them. She tried not to think about what she saw, but the more she tried to suppress her thoughts, the more preoccupied by the images she became. She told me, "The images seemed to take over my mind. I felt contaminated by whatever I had encountered, and I felt the need to run home and shower with very hot water."

Responsibility for Harm or Mistakes

Most people don't want to be irresponsible or make mistakes and would feel horrible if something bad happened to people, especially those they love, because of something they did or didn't do. This type of obsession involves thoughts about being responsible for something bad happening, either because of not doing enough to prevent it or due to making mistakes that cause it. Common responsibility obsessions include *What if I left the stove on and my house burns down? What if I left the door unlocked and intruders harm my family? What if the bump I felt while driving to work was a pedestrian I hit with my car?* Again, these kinds of thoughts aren't unusual; many people have them. But if you struggle with this type of OCD, your doubts stick and make you highly anxious.

Ted agonized about decisions that involved potential responsibility for harm. He couldn't let go of thoughts such as *Did I see broken glass in the park today and not pick it up? Maybe I missed a piece of broken glass and a barefooted child will step on it. It will be my fault. And what if I'm responsible for all airline disasters since I retired because I didn't write a report about something I overheard one day?* Ted felt responsible for possible misfortunes that could have occurred or that might occur because of oversights or mistakes he might have made. He didn't want to think about these possibilities and didn't want to keep questioning his actions. He knew that his concerns weren't rational, yet he couldn't ignore them. They kept returning. Ted felt the weight of the world on his shoulders.

Symmetry, Order, or Completeness

Some obsessions focus on excessive desires for symmetry, orderliness, or feelings of completion. For example, you may feel that if you touch something with one hand, you must also touch it with your other hand. You may feel the need to complete a task or read every word of an article before you leave it. You may want books to line up on shelves in certain ways or in the right order. Of course, "certain ways" or "the right order" will mean different things to different people. For people with

OCD, this is based on recurrent thoughts about how things should be, and the logic may not appear obvious to others.

If tasks aren't performed "exactly right" or completed, sometimes in a ritualized fashion, you may feel highly anxious. For example, you may have thoughts like *I must rub shampoo into my hair twenty times exactly* or *I need to tap my toothbrush four times before and after brushing my teeth and use four pumps of soap when I wash my hands.* If your routine is disrupted or isn't completed, you may feel quite distressed.

People without OCD may have preferences for symmetry, orderliness, or completeness, but these are simply preferences: choices they want to make. They don't involve intrusive, unwanted thoughts that it's necessary to line up items symmetrically or complete tasks in a certain order to avoid high levels of distress.

If you have this type of OCD, you wish it didn't feel intolerable when actions aren't done "just so" or items don't line up "just right." If symmetry, order, or completeness can't be achieved, you might fear dire consequences. For example, you might think *If I don't tap two times with my right hand and two times with my left hand, my grandfather might die.* You recognize that such thoughts aren't rational, yet they pop into your head and trigger such tremendous discomfort and anxiety that they can feel real. Alternatively, you may not fear specific consequences and instead fear experiencing levels of discomfort that seem almost impossible to bear. Clients often tell me, "I'm not afraid of anything specific happening if I don't do things 'just right,' but I'll feel too uncomfortable if I don't."

Aggressive Thoughts

Sometimes violent images pop into people's heads. Thoughts about doing something harmful or inappropriate may cross anyone's mind. If we're honest, we all have disturbing thoughts. But if you suffer from this type of OCD, these disturbing thoughts and images can be terrifying. The distress they provoke feels unbearable, and the uncertainty and doubt they trigger feel intolerable. You may feel tormented by wondering what having these thoughts mean about you. You may conclude that you must be a horrible person because you have horrible thoughts.

You desperately want these disturbing thoughts and images to go away because they go against the grain of who you are and what you value.

If you have this type of OCD, you can be tormented by thoughts of possibly losing control and doing horrible things. You might have thoughts like these:

◆ *What if I lose control and stab my spouse with a knife from the kitchen?*

◆ *If I have scary images of harming my child, could it mean I might do it?*

◆ *Could I lose control and strangle my cat?*

◆ *What if I suddenly lose control and push an elderly person off the subway platform?*

◆ *If a racist thought enters my mind, could I blurt it out even though it's the last thing I'd ever want to say?*

◆ *Could I suddenly act on an impulse and jump into traffic?*

Clients often ask me, "How can I know for sure that I won't do such a thing? How do you know for certain that I won't?" Aggressive obsessions trigger almost unbearable doubt and endless self-questioning. You fear your thoughts and find them abhorrent. When Gina was young, she was terrified by obsessive thoughts and wondered if she was capable of murdering her entire family. She cried in bed at night, hoping the thoughts would stop. After the birth of her daughter, she was tormented by obsessive thoughts about whether she could kill her. This OCD subtype isn't as easily portrayed in media as types that involve fears about germs, leaving doors unlocked, or not tapping items a certain number of times. This can make it especially isolating to suffer from this type of OCD.

If you suffer from this type of OCD, you fear that having a violent thought could mean you're capable of committing a violent act or that you're somehow bad because you have such a thought. It can feel frightening to talk about these fears. You may fear that others will judge you, think you might be dangerous, and maybe even call the police. Popular culture does not yet portray how people with OCD misinterpret unwanted disturbing thoughts. Therefore, it's possible that people who don't know you well or who are uninformed about OCD may misinterpret your concerns as you fear they might. With greater efforts underway to inform people about all types of OCD, you may feel less reluctant to tell others about your fears, while, of course, choosing your confidants wisely.

Sexual Thoughts

Obsessions can take the form of unwanted sexual thoughts and images. These can feel highly disturbing, but they aren't unusual. Many people have such thoughts. Plus, having thoughts doesn't mean acting on thoughts. Nevertheless, similar to aggressive obsessions, these obsessions can involve unrelenting self-questioning and extreme anxiety about whether you could commit certain acts, such as *How can I be sure I won't molest a child?* or *What if I lose control and do something sexually perverse?*

A type of sexual obsession, *sexual orientation obsessions*, involves doubts about one's sexual orientation. These aren't intentional thoughts about your sexual identity. They're unwanted thoughts that cause great anguish because of unrelenting doubt. Whether you're straight or gay, you might question if you could have the other sexual orientation. You might be straight but fear that you could become gay. You might feel tormented by not knowing how you can ever be sure about your sexual orientation. Gina described how her obsessions flip-flopped between violent, aggressive thoughts of harming people she loved and obsessions questioning whether she was gay. She knew she wasn't gay, yet she was tormented by wondering how she could ever know for sure. She was terrified to work alongside attractive female colleagues because she thought their presence might trigger an onslaught of obsessions. People with these obsessions often fear being misunderstood. They know their sexual orientation and don't understand why their doubts won't stop.

Moral and Religious Thoughts

Scrupulosity involves thoughts and doubts about violating religious and moral codes. Blasphemous thoughts are especially disturbing to people with strong religious convictions. Unwanted thoughts about committing a sin can trigger agonizing distress. Yet you can't control the thoughts or images that enter your mind. And with OCD, thoughts and images tend to stick in spite of desperate efforts not to have them. Ted was tormented by sinful thoughts and unrelenting questions about how he could know if his intentions to become a priest were pure.

You don't need to be religious to have obsessions about morality. Many people try to do the right thing and live by certain moral codes. When faced with dilemmas about "right" and "wrong" behaviors, most people try to act with integrity. If you have obsessions about morality, doubts about your behaviors or thoughts being immoral or wrong can cause great anguish. Doubts about whether you're a good person or have pure intentions can trigger endless attempts to gain certainty. You may feel tormented by thoughts like *Was I completely honest when I talked to my boyfriend about my past?* or *How do I know if I truly am a good person or if I'm just acting like one?*

Relationships

Doubts about romantic relationships are not unusual, but obsessions involve a preoccupation with them and often interfere with relationships themselves. These obsessions can include several themes (Doron et al. 2012): questioning feelings toward one's partner (*How can I know for sure that I love my partner?*), questioning your partner's fidelity and feelings for you (*How do I know for sure that my partner is faithful and loves me?*), and appraisals of the relationship (*How can I know if my partner is the one for me?*). Obsessive jealousy and questioning your partner's feelings and actions can put great strain on your relationship. Excessive doubts about your own feelings and about your relationship may leave you stuck and unable to commit to your partner. Gina not only felt consumed by obsessions about her sexual orientation, but also felt exhausted by her unrelenting quest for certainty about her feelings for her husband. Links between sexual orientation obsessions and relationship doubts are not uncommon (Doron, Derby, and Szepsenwol in press).

EXERCISE: Identifying Your Obsessions

You can probably relate to some or many of the obsessions discussed above, or you may suffer from intrusive thoughts, urges, or images that I haven't described. Obsessions take many forms. No matter what their content, obsessions are intrusive, unwanted, and disturbing. That's what they all have in common. You don't want to have them, but they keep returning. The content of obsessions isn't different from what most people sometimes think or imagine, but if you have OCD, these thoughts stick and cause you great distress.

Identifying your obsessions is a key part of treatment. Since treatment involves learning to face obsessions without engaging in compulsions, it's important to clarify what your obsessions are and what you fear will happen if you don't use compulsions. This is how you personalize ERP to fit your symptoms. I encourage you to write your answers to the following questions in your journal. This list need not be "perfect"! You can always come back and add to it later. You'll discuss the content of your obsessions in detail when you meet with your therapist. Writing them down now, though, is a great way to start understanding your symptoms.

- What recurrent, intrusive, and unwanted thoughts, urges, or images make you anxious or distressed?

- Do your obsessions involve contamination concerns; responsibility for harm or mistakes; needs for symmetry, orderliness, or completion; aggressive, sexual, or morality themes; or doubts about relationships? Do they involve other types of concerns?

- Do your thoughts fit primarily into one category, or do they fall into more than one category?

- What are the feared consequences of these thoughts, urges, or images that cause you to feel distressed? Are you afraid that something bad might happen? Do you fear feeling so anxious or uncomfortable that you won't be able to function? Are you afraid that your thoughts might mean something bad about you?

Underlying Themes

Given the varied content of obsessions, you may wonder why they all indicate the same disorder: OCD. Learning about the common themes underlying OCD will help you understand what lies at the heart of your problem and what different types of OCD have in common. OCD symptoms are associated with certain beliefs, and these beliefs center around themes that include perfectionism and intolerance of uncertainty, inflated responsibility and overestimating threat, and interpreting thoughts as overly important and believing it's important to control them (Obsessive Compulsive Cognitions Working Group 2005). A common theme that helps maintain OCD is underestimating your ability to cope with anxiety or distress. Obsessions may have different and sometimes very personal and idiosyncratic content, but when you target the themes underlying them, you target the core problem. As you read this section, consider how these themes might be at play in the expression of your symptoms.

Intolerance of Uncertainty

People with OCD have difficulty tolerating uncertainty. Given that you struggle with OCD, you undoubtedly know how true this is! Most people don't like having doubts or feeling uncertain, but when you have OCD, alleviating doubts and finding certainty can feel like a life-or-death matter. Coping with the uncertainty triggered by obsessions is a core problem in OCD: *If I touch this table, could I become contaminated by a deadly disease? Did I remember to be sure that the knobs on the stove were turned off before I left the house? If I have an image of picking up a kitchen knife and stabbing my spouse, how do I know I won't do it? How do I know that my intentions were pure when I took my marriage vows? If I don't tap the table in counts of three, maybe something bad might happen.* The belief that uncertainty is too hard to tolerate is a major problem for people with OCD.

Perfectionism or Wanting Things to Be "Just Right"

Being a perfectionist doesn't necessarily mean you suffer from OCD. Striving to do well and get things right can be motivating. And while it can be detrimental, if excessive people who don't suffer from OCD can usually move on if things don't look or feel perfect, whereas with OCD, you may feel that if you don't do things perfectly or in a certain way, dire consequences could occur that would be your fault. You may fear that you can't handle the discomfort that you'll feel if you don't achieve that "just right" feeling. Uncertainty can prevent you from achieving a sense of perfection, and that can feel intolerable. The urge to make things "just right" can feel overwhelming.

Inflated Sense of Responsibility and Overestimating Threats

Some obsessions involve inflated beliefs about your level of responsibility. You might feel a great degree of responsibility to safeguard others by avoiding oversights and never making mistakes. You may attempt to prevent possible catastrophic consequences by trying to do everything "just right." You might feel overly responsible for protecting others from accidental dangers, such as a home fire or burglary, or from contamination. People with OCD also overestimate the likelihood and severity of certain threats. If you have contamination obsessions, you probably overestimate the likelihood of threat from exposure to places, people, or objects that cause you to feel contaminated. Uncertainty about remembering to lock a door or turn off the stove tends to feel especially threatening due to the potentially disastrous consequences if you make a mistake.

Interpreting Thoughts as Overly Important and Believing It's Important to Control Them

People with OCD tend to interpret intrusive thoughts as especially important. When you believe that certain thoughts must be important, these thoughts grab your attention. *Thought-action fusion* is a term that describes giving certain thoughts too much importance (Rachman 1993). You may believe that having unwanted thoughts means you could act on them, or you may believe that having a thought is the moral equivalent of acting on it. You may fear that if you have a thought, it could occur. If you have an intrusive thought about stabbing the person next to you, you might interpret it as meaning you could be a murderer. You might conclude that you must be a bad person because you have bad thoughts.

If you view intrusive thoughts as important and threatening, it makes sense that you'd want to control them and stop having them. Unfortunately, the more you try to control thoughts, the less in control you feel. Attempts to suppress unwanted thoughts typically have a paradoxical effect, actually increasing the frequency of those thoughts (Wegner et al. 1987). Have you ever tried not to think about something? What usually happens? The more you try not to think about something, the more it enters your mind. Trying to control and suppress thoughts doesn't work, and efforts to do so only make the thoughts seem more significant.

Underestimation of Ability to Cope with Anxiety or Discomfort

You may think you can't handle the level of anxiety or distress that results from your obsessions. When uncertainty and feelings of threat or responsibility arise, it can feel intolerable. If something doesn't seem just right, you may feel extremely uncomfortable. It may seem nearly impossible to cope with frightening obsessive thoughts. Obsessions can feel overwhelming, to say the least. People with OCD often ask, "How can I simply ride out these feelings when the threat feels so real? How can I cope with feeling like I might be responsible for something horrible happening to people I love?" If you have questions like these, you probably feel at a loss about what to do. If the thoughts and images seem highly threatening and you don't think you can cope with them, it's natural to feel anxious and want to seek relief. Although this underlying theme isn't specific to OCD and applies to many disorders, it plays an important role in understanding why you use compulsions or avoidance when your obsessions are triggered.

EXERCISE: Identifying Underlying Themes

Identifying the themes that underlie your OCD will help you know what you're up against when learning to face your fears, instead of using compulsions or avoidance to feel better. Once you understand the problems that lie at the heart of your symptoms, you'll be in a good position to take on the challenges that lie ahead. You'll know what your real challenge entails: facing the underlying themes of your obsessions no matter what their content. In your journal, write your responses to the following questions and include examples; this will help you identify the underlying OCD themes most relevant to you.

- How does uncertainty play a role in your symptoms? Is it hard for you to tolerate uncertainty? Do you wish you could just feel certain about what makes you anxious or uncomfortable and think that would make everything okay?

- If certain things aren't perfect or just right, or if you don't achieve that "just so" feeling, does it seem almost impossible to bear? Do you feel overwhelmed and uncomfortable if you can't make some things look or feel just right?

- Do you tend to feel overly responsible for preventing negative outcomes? Do you overestimate the likelihood or severity of threats more than other people seem to do?

- Do some thoughts frighten you because they seem abhorrent or disturbing to you? Do you interpret them as especially important?

Do you believe it's important to be able to control them? Do they cause you to worry that you could do something horrible or embarrassing? Do you think you might be a bad person because you have "bad" thoughts?

♦ Do your obsessions seem too anxiety provoking or distressing to tolerate? Do you feel the need to seek immediate relief? Do you think you might underestimate your ability to cope with the anxiety and distress? What do you fear will happen if you can't stop your thoughts or find relief from your fears and doubts?

What Are Compulsions?

Compulsions are defined as repetitive behaviors or mental acts that are either carried out in response to obsessions or based on rigid rules that you feel the need to follow (American Psychiatric Association 2013). When you have OCD, you may engage in repetitive behaviors, or *rituals*, such as hand washing or checking, usually with rigid rules about exactly how to do them. You may engage in mental rituals, such as repeating certain phrases or numbers in your head with the hope of decreasing your anxiety or the likelihood of something bad happening. You may mentally review your actions to be certain you've done everything correctly. Compulsions are attempts to reduce anxiety or distress or prevent negative events, yet they aren't realistic solutions and are often quite excessive. In addition, they are time-consuming and become additional sources of distress.

It makes sense that you would respond to distress caused by obsessions by engaging in behaviors that might provide some relief. Compulsions are often fueled by thoughts along these lines: *If I go back and check to see if the stove is off, I'll feel reassured. If I wash my hands again and do it in a certain way, I'll feel free from contamination. If I can convince myself that I would never harm my spouse or child, I'll feel better.* Make sense? It would if we could ever know anything for certain. That's the problem in OCD: you can never achieve the complete certainty you seek. In spite of your best efforts to obtain certainty, achieve that "just right" feeling, decrease a sense of threat or responsibility, or try to control your thoughts, you only achieve some short-term relief. If you're afraid of certain thoughts, urges, or images, you'll experience distress when you have them, try harder to get rid of them, and then experience them more frequently, creating a vicious cycle.

Like obsessions, compulsions generally fall into categories, and certain compulsions are often paired with certain obsessions. For example, washing compulsions are frequently used in response to contamination obsessions, and checking compulsions are used to alleviate doubts about responsibility for harm or mistakes. However, there can be a lot of crossover, and it's also common to perform compulsions from more than one category. For example, you might have contamination obsessions and engage in both washing and checking rituals. Because compulsions are responses to specific obsessions, they can be quite specific. While one person may check to be sure he didn't accidentally harm anyone, another may check to be sure she didn't come into contact with dirt. Yet even when compulsive behaviors look quite different on the outside, they all serve a common function: attempting to decrease anxiety and distress in response to the activation of underlying OCD themes.

Washing and Cleaning

Excessive hand washing, showering, and cleaning, often done in ritualized ways, are examples of decontamination compulsions. Excessive washing and cleaning rituals are attempts to get rid of terrible feelings of anxiety or disgust when you feel like you've been exposed to possible contaminants or disturbing images, places, or people. Mary felt the need to shower after work, riding the bus, using dirty restrooms, and being anywhere that didn't feel clean to her. She also showered after seeing things that disturbed her. Her washing and cleaning compulsions often were responses to feeling contaminated due to associations with disturbing images. She didn't need to touch anything to feel contaminated and want to shower.

Checking

You may repeatedly check to be certain you didn't cause harm or make a mistake. You might circle back to check intersections to be sure you didn't harm a pedestrian or animal when driving. You might go through lengthy checking rituals before leaving the house to feel certain that appliances are unplugged, windows are closed, and doors are locked. Checking rituals eat up a lot of valuable time and can result in feeling exhausted before you even leave home. Ted did a lot of checking. He took responsibility for being the "glass police" and checked for fragments of broken glass in streets and parks. His nephews couldn't understand why he searched for glass fragments everywhere he went. They didn't know that he feared being responsible for a child accidentally stepping on a piece of glass because he hadn't been vigilant.

Making Things "Just Right"

Some compulsions involve ordering or arranging items in certain ways, often to achieve symmetry, orderliness, or completion and that "just right" feeling. You may spend inordinate amounts of time arranging items at home, at work, or even in public places until it feels like they're lined up correctly. You may have rules about the order in which routine activities must be completed. If that order is interrupted or you aren't sure you adhered to the right order, you may feel the need to start over. You may rewrite sentences or paragraphs to get the words to line up just so on the page. You may repeat routine activities, such as going through doorways, or body movements, such as tapping your foot a certain number of times, in attempts to feel just right.

When Gina was a child, before she had aggressive and violent intrusive thoughts, she repeatedly tapped things in ritualized ways. Her compulsions had a superstitious quality. Here's how she described her early experiences:

During the fourth grade I was sitting at my desk when an overwhelming urge came over me to tap underneath my desk an even number of times. I didn't understand why I felt this urge or why I felt so much distress. All I knew was that I had to carry out this compulsion or something bad might happen to people I love. I don't remember exactly how many times I had to tap, but it would have been an even number, with the exception of the number six. I thought odd numbers were bad. The number six was bad too because that was the devil's number. I carried a heavy burden for the well-being of those close to me, and it was my responsibility to carry out these compulsions to make sure that nothing bad would happen to them.

Compulsions can involve attempts to understand things perfectly. You might repeatedly read paragraphs in books or entire newspaper or magazine articles to be certain you understand everything you read. An especially troubling obsession is the need to know exactly what loved ones did in the past and why they made certain choices. Of course, no matter how many ways you try to find answers, you don't obtain 100 percent certainty, and in the absence of certainty, things don't feel just right.

Mental Rituals

Mental rituals occur in your head rather than as outwardly observable behaviors. Other people can't see you performing these rituals. They involve behaviors like counting in certain ways while performing tasks or "undoing" a bad thought by replacing it with a good one. Since outward checking behaviors aren't always possible, you might spend time mentally retracing your steps in an effort to feel certain that you did indeed turn off the stove or that you didn't touch a "contaminated" towel in the laundry basket. If you think about a "bad" thought or number, you can't really take it back, but you can try to undo it by thinking or saying something good. For example, if the word "devil" enters your mind, you might mentally repeat certain words you deem to be good, such as "angel," or if you think about a "bad" number, you might count to a certain lucky number.

Reassurance Seeking

Seeking reassurance is another behavior used in the quest for certainty. You may repeatedly search for information on the Internet or ask questions of family members, friends, or professionals about the likelihood of contamination, or of your mistakenly causing harm. Confessing any possible wrongdoing can be used in an attempt to gain reassurance that you're an honest person. Mary sought reassurance by searching the Internet to decrease her feelings of uncertainty about troubling things she might have seen. Ted sought reassurance by mentally reviewing details of baptisms, weddings, and last rites that he'd performed to be certain that he didn't make mistakes. When that wasn't enough, he checked with witnesses and his superior in efforts to gain reassurance. Gina tried to reassure herself that she couldn't possibly be capable of murdering her family by engaging in countless hours of mental reassurance seeking. She also tried to reassure herself that she wasn't attracted to women.

Avoidance

Avoiding thoughts and situations that trigger them is a strategy used to minimize the likelihood of feeling anxious and engaging in rituals. Probably all of my clients try to avoid triggering obsessions. They may change routes to work, quit their jobs, avoid interactions with children, or even move out of their homes in desperate attempts to escape the triggers of their obsessions and anxiety. Once obsessions are triggered, it can feel like everything becomes spoiled, including the rest of your day or even your life, if you don't find the certainty or reassurance you seek. Therefore, avoidance may seem like a logical preventative measure; but it comes with a high cost.

Mary gave up an important friendship because she wanted to avoid triggering anxiety and disgust. Her friend Connie found something indistinguishable in the sink drain of her new apartment and described it to her. Mary told me about how the image affected her: "Whatever Connie had found in her drain was in my mind to stay. I began a compulsive cycle trying to get rid of the image of a stringy, slimy, white thing with teeth. I couldn't figure it out by searching the Internet. I tried to avoid the thoughts and images by washing, working, and sweating at the gym, but ultimately I had to give up my friend Connie. I couldn't be around her, let alone ever consider seeing her new apartment." Mary also almost didn't audition for a play for similar reasons. When she learned where the auditions were being held, she desperately wanted to avoid the building because she had seen mouse droppings there before. She went for the audition but tried to avoid areas where she feared seeing anything that would trigger her obsessions and compulsions, which made it difficult for her to focus on why she was there.

If you fear that having horrible thoughts might mean you'll do something horrible, you're probably tempted to avoid people and situations not only because you fear triggering obsessions and anxiety, but also because you fear you might act on your thoughts. Gina tried to avoid being around her family, especially her sister and young cousins, when she feared that intrusive thoughts about harming family members meant she might be capable of actually harming them. When she had her own child, she desperately tried to avoid triggering her harming fears. Gina told me, "The biggest trigger for thoughts of harming my baby was bath time. Just the thought that my daughter needed a bath caused me a great deal of anxiety. My mind would race with thoughts like *What if I just lose it and hold her head underwater this time?*" Gina avoided being alone while bathing her baby. At other times, she tried to avoid female friends because she feared triggering obsessions about her sexual orientation.

You may avoid standing near people because you fear triggering thoughts of pushing them into harm's way, such as into traffic or in front of an oncoming subway train. You might avoid going to bed due to fears of having violent thoughts that you could harm your spouse if you wake up groggy during the night. My clients frequently report that they avoid knives in the kitchen due to fears of triggering intrusive thoughts about killing family members. Avoidance is a common strategy no matter what the content of obsessions or compulsions.

Compulsions and avoidance behaviors are sometimes called *safety behaviors* because they strengthen the belief that using them keeps you safe—that if you hadn't used them, you might have suffered from unwanted and dangerous consequences (Salkovskis 1991). But when you use them, you don't learn that feared negative outcomes are highly unlikely.

Sometimes safety behaviors can be quite subtle. For example, if you fear touching something dirty, you may strategically use a tissue when picking it up or only carry it with your fingertips and make sure not to touch anything else until you can wash your hands. If you have a negative thought, you may mentally repeat positive thoughts to ward off dangers from negative ones. In this way, you perceive your behaviors as keeping you safe from the dreaded consequences of exposure to certain objects or thoughts.

EXERCISE: Identifying Your Compulsions and Avoidance Behaviors

Identifying your compulsions and avoidance behaviors is an important step in your recovery. When you engage in ERP, you'll need to be very clear about the specifics of these behaviors so you can practice **not** engaging in them when confronting situations that trigger your obsessions. In your journal, write your responses to the following questions, which will help you identify your compulsions and avoidance behaviors:

◆ What compulsions do you use to seek relief from the distress caused by your obsessions? Do you wash, clean, check, mentally check, repeat, try to "undo" thoughts, or seek reassurance?

◆ Do you try to avoid situations that trigger your obsessions? What do you try to avoid? Do you avoid certain people, places, or situations? Do you try to avoid certain thoughts?

◆ How effective are your compulsions and avoidance behaviors? Do they work in the short term?

◆ Do compulsions and avoidance provide relief in the long run? Have they made your problems better or worse?

Why Compulsions and Avoidance Strategies Don't Work

Compulsions and avoidance can provide a temporary fix. Initially, they may offer some relief, but unfortunately, that relief is fleeting. You can go home and check to be sure the door is locked. You can drive back to where you think you felt a bump and check to see if a pedestrian is lying on the road. You can wash your hands ten times. You can seek reassurance that you aren't the type of person who commits murder. You can try to avoid triggers of obsessions. And if you do these things, you might feel better. You might feel reassured, at least for a while. But what happens when problematic thoughts return? You're likely to think, *Am I sure that the door is locked? Could I have missed seeing someone on the road? Am I certain that I'm not contaminated? How can I know for sure that I won't harm someone someday?* Compulsions and avoidance never relieve all doubt. You can never achieve absolute certainty.

"Why Me?"

You may wonder why some people have more difficulty tolerating uncertainty and other underlying themes of OCD. You may ask, "Why me?" The answer isn't known for sure, but genetic and biological vulnerabilities may play a role. Learning can also play a role, as people develop associations between negative emotions and certain triggers. For example, if one unclean public restroom triggers anxiety or disgust, then other public restrooms can become associated with anxiety or disgust. In addition, certain behaviors can be reinforced. By avoiding public restrooms or washing excessively after using one, you might prevent or reduce anxiety in the short term—which is reinforcing, and means you'll be more likely to engage in the same behaviors in the future. With time, strategies to reduce or avoid distress can generalize to other places, making you more likely to use avoidance or compulsions when you encounter other triggers that are similar.

Summary

Obsessions are intrusive, unwanted, and recurrent thoughts, urges, or images that cause high levels of anxiety and distress. Compulsions are repetitive behaviors or mental rituals aimed at reducing anxiety and distress. Avoidance is a strategy to minimize the likelihood of encountering situations that trigger obsessions and urges to engage in compulsions. Unfortunately, compulsions and avoidance only provide temporary relief; they don't provide the certainty and reassurance you seek.

What's most important to understand is that obsessions are expressions of underlying themes. These themes are the real problems, and you must face them without using compulsions to manage anxiety and distress. The content of obsessions and compulsions can vary, sometimes looking worlds apart to outside observers and even to people with OCD. Yet whatever form your OCD symptoms take, and no matter how different your symptoms seem to be from those of another person, you have a lot in common with others who suffer from OCD. You struggle with underlying themes such as intolerance of uncertainty, perfectionism and wanting things to be "just right," overestimations of responsibility or threat, and interpreting thoughts as important and necessary to control. It's likely that you also underestimate your ability to cope with the anxiety and distress triggered by obsessions.

In chapter 2, I'll explain how you probably got into this predicament. I'll discuss the OCD cycle, how it begins, and how it strengthens its hold. A core difficulty in OCD is problematic efforts to cope with distress triggered by the underlying themes described in this chapter. Treatment teaches you to respond to those themes without using compulsions or seeking reassurance. Understanding how you got caught in the OCD cycle paves the way for understanding what you need to do to break it.

CHAPTER 2

THE OCD CYCLE

OCD often begins with seemingly harmless responses to disturbing thoghts or images. It feels intuitive to check the stove if you think you might have left a burner on, to wash your hands if you think you were exposed to germs, or to ask a question one more time to be certain you understand the answer. If you have an image of harming someone and it frightens you, it probably seems natural to do what you can to rid yourself of the image. These kinds of behaviors can seem innocent enough when they aren't frequent or pervasive. And in fact, most clients tell me they can look back and see early signs of OCD that appeared long before their symptoms blossomed into full-blown problems. They didn't think much of them at the time.

OCD symptoms can develop over the course of years or, in some cases, in a very short time. Typically, symptoms gradually worsen. There are exceptions, such as a sudden onset or worsening of symptoms in childhood thought to be related to immune reactions to infection, including pediatric autoimmune neuropsychiatric disorder associated with streptococcal infections (PANDAS). Perinatal or postpartum OCD also involves a sudden onset or worsening of symptoms, in this case in women shortly before or after giving birth. But for many people with OCD, symptoms progressively intensify and seem to morph into different thoughts and behaviors over time.

At the outset of therapy, a therapist will ask for a description of your problems, review your personal history, ascertain how OCD affects your life, and probably ask you to complete measures to assess your symptoms and their severity. In just one or two sessions, a therapist may be able to encapsulate years of suffering, discuss your OCD symptoms, and recommend a treatment plan. But a good therapist understands that your story isn't just a checklist of symptoms, and recognizes that your struggle with OCD has been a part of your life, probably for a long time.

You may feel confused or embarrassed by your symptoms. You may feel that your thoughts or behaviors are unusual and unique to you. You may worry that your therapist can't possibly understand the way you think or the things you do, or that your therapist won't appreciate the depth of your suffering and the intensity of your battles with obsessions and compulsions. It is true that your particular case of OCD is one of a kind and your symptoms are unique to you. But as you learned in chapter 1, your symptoms also share common themes with those of others who suffer from OCD. In addition, the progression of your symptoms may look similar to that of others with OCD.

When your symptoms began, you might not have seen them as a problem. Many people with OCD don't recognize their symptoms as such for quite some time. If it has taken you a while to seek treatment, you are not alone. A therapist specializing in treating OCD will understand why you may have hesitated before seeking treatment and will understand how your symptoms may have crept up on you. The OCD cycle takes hold as your thoughts feel threatening and your behaviors strengthen their grip on you. Obsessions and compulsions may start to change and morph, but the underlying OCD themes remain. At some point, you probably found yourself stuck in OCD cycles and too frightened to break them, and your symptoms began taking a toll not just on you but also on those you love. An OCD specialist understands the OCD cycle and can help you break it.

Early Signs

You may remember signs of OCD that showed up in your childhood or adolescence. Sometimes early symptoms are noticeable to parents, teachers, and friends, but they often go unrecognized. You may have sensed that your thoughts and behaviors seemed unusual, or you might have felt that they were just part of who you were. Maybe you remember performing rituals that felt harmless early on but now feel out of control and hard to resist.

When Mary was in college, she cleaned her cat's litter box first thing when she woke up. Whenever the litter box looked dirty, she felt uneasy and immediately felt the need to scoop. But scooping never felt like enough, so she completely emptied the box and scrubbed it in the sink with dish soap. She used a sponge that she reserved only for the litter box. After putting fresh litter in the box, she felt an urge to mop the floor. Even if she was running late to class, she mopped the floor first.

Mary would work on autopilot. She would automatically fill the bucket from underneath the sink with hot water and a few tablespoons of Pine-Sol. She mopped the dining room floor first because that's where she kept the litter box. She would mop the entire floor, but go over the area where the litter box sat repeatedly. Then she'd wash the clothes she'd been wearing because they felt dirty after cleaning the floor and litter box area. She often washed her sheets too, to be sure they stayed clean. Before going to the washing machine in the basement, she'd put on a special robe, the only article of clothing that she allowed to touch her skin before she felt clean. This was her preshower morning ritual.

Mary's morning routine seemed natural to her. She told me, "When I felt the urge to clean, it was automatic, like an itch I was scratching. The morning mopping ritual felt no different than brushing my teeth. I would go through a bottle of Pine-Sol every few weeks." Mary didn't think her behaviors were symptoms of OCD—at least not yet.

Gina realized that some of her behaviors were different as early as elementary school, when she started doing tapping rituals to prevent something terrible from happening. Soon after, she started repeatedly checking to be sure that home appliances were turned off and began washing her hands frequently to be sure she was germ-free. She felt the need to confess if she thought that she had done anything bad. Gina tried to hide her behaviors. She told me, "I knew that what I did caused me great anxiety and wasn't normal. I knew that it didn't make sense. I worried about what people would think of me if they knew why I did what I did, so I went to great lengths to hide it. My mom just thought I was conscientious and wanted to do things just right."

Ted told me that he remembered early OCD symptoms during college when he was studying to be ordained as a priest: "It felt like my brain started playing tricks. I kept feeling like I'd done something wrong—something I had to correct. If I scratched a cabinet, I'd immediately think, *I need to report it to the superior!* Sometimes I couldn't remember doing anything wrong, but if I had a bad thought, I'd worry that maybe I *did* do something. OCD is like that. You think a bad thought and then you make it seem like a reality."

Ted's early obsessions involved scrupulosity. Memories of childhood wrongdoings tormented him. As he explained it, "I was going to be a priest, and I needed to clear the record and be sure I'd been forgiven for everything. I agonized about past sins and sinful thoughts. Just having an impure thought felt like a sin, but I couldn't stop my thoughts." Ted usually struggled in silence. No one realized how much he suffered. He told me, "I like to believe that I was completely hiding any symptoms, but early on I didn't even recognize my symptoms. I just thought I wasn't able to live up to standards that others could easily meet. I only recognized my overreactions as symptoms when I learned about OCD later in life."

Looking at the early symptoms Mary, Gina, and Ted experienced, it may seem obvious that they struggled with obsessions and engaged in compulsions. Yet to them, even if their thoughts and behaviors were annoying or time-consuming, those thoughts and behaviors were a part of their lives. Early symptoms of OCD often creep up on you bit by bit. This has been called the "creep-up factor." Symptoms don't always seem like cause for alarm or trigger a call to the doctor, at least not initially.

Because OCD symptoms often begin insidiously and creep up slowly, it can be hard to recognize when you have a problem and need treatment. You may have tried to keep your OCD a secret for a long time. If you've felt embarrassed by your symptoms and have become accustomed to hiding them, seeking help may feel hard to do. I hope that understanding how OCD symptoms often begin will help you realize that you aren't alone. For most people, these problems develop over time. If it took some time before you realized you had a problem that warranted treatment, that's understandable.

EXERCISE: Understanding Your Early Signs of OCD

Remembering the early signs of OCD in your life will help you understand how your problem began. While it's not necessary to pinpoint exactly when your thoughts and behaviors became symptoms of a disorder, many clients find it helpful to understand how their early behaviors set the stage for their current problems. When you see how your OCD symptoms began, they'll start to make more sense. Your symptoms didn't just come out of the blue; they probably started a long time ago and strengthened gradually as you engaged in compulsions. Understanding how symptoms creep up on you helps you understand how detrimental engaging in compulsions can be, even when they seem relatively harmless. In your journal, write down whatever you remember about your early signs of OCD, using the following questions for guidance:

◆ Do you remember early intrusive and repetitive thoughts, urges, or images? How did you respond to them? Did you use compulsions, seek reassurance, or avoid triggering them?

◆ How did your initial OCD symptoms affect your life? Did your thoughts make you anxious? Did your behaviors become time-consuming?

◆ Were you skilled at hiding your compulsions? Did your thoughts and behaviors seem harmless, or did you think you were different from others or worry that something was wrong with you?

Thoughts Become Threatening

People without OCD can usually dismiss pesky thoughts, urges, or images. They may find some thoughts disturbing but not view them as especially important. Most people might question whether something is dirty or whether they could lose control and commit an unwanted act, but they're generally able to let those questions go. Their unpleasant emotions dissipate quickly. Walking past a knife on the counter might evoke an image of stabbing someone, but most people can quickly dismiss the image and move on with whatever they were doing.

Thoughts and images become threatening when they're interpreted as important. Our bodies respond to high levels of threat by activating the fight-or-flight response, which puts us on high alert. Of course, thoughts and mental images don't pose real threats, but if you interpret them as important, dangerous, or intolerable, you'll be on high alert in response to them. Mary's therapist described a metaphor that helped her understand how her body reacted to certain obsessions. He told her a story about seeing a garden hose on the ground and mistaking it for a snake. Mary explained it to me like this: "My OCD brain processes all the garden hoses of the world as snakes. So when I see something that spikes my OCD, typically a dirty toilet or anything disgusting, I don't see it for what it is. I see it as something to fear, and that sends a message to my brain to run and avoid it. The brain sends signals to help us react appropriately to fear. But with OCD, there's a hijacking of sorts that goes on between the brain signals."

You may be triggered by contamination thoughts, whereas someone else is triggered by unwanted sexual or aggressive thoughts, or by thoughts of accidentally causing harm or not completing tasks in just the right order. People with OCD seem to be disturbed by intrusive thoughts associated with what they value or deem to be important. Contamination thoughts are threatening if you value cleanliness. Racist thoughts are threatening if you value social justice. Blasphemous thoughts are threatening if you value religious codes. When you have OCD and your intrusive thoughts aren't in line with your values, you can perceive them as threatening.

Just like a garden hose, thoughts, urges, or images aren't especially frightening to most people. It's smart to be wary of germs and contaminants. It's wise to be responsible about turning off the stove and locking doors. It's helpful to want a degree of orderliness in life. It isn't desirable to cause harm to others. Obsessive thoughts aren't "crazy." Remember, the content of obsessions isn't different from what most people may think or imagine. But when you have OCD, certain thoughts seem especially important and can even trigger a fight-or-flight response. You may feel as though you're facing an emergency or life-or-death situation.

Your own thoughts become a source of threat and dread and create a sense of urgency to quickly do something to suppress them or reduce risks associated with them.

Compulsions Strengthen the OCD Cycle

In response to threatening thoughts, you probably started to do what seemed natural: decontaminate, check in an attempt to gain certainty, "undo" bad thoughts by replacing them with good ones, seek reassurance, or avoid triggering distress altogether. It's likely that you used a range of safety behaviors to feel better and avoid the perceived negative consequences of your thoughts. You wanted your disturbing thoughts to go away, and you wanted to feel certain that everything was safe. You probably did whatever you could to seek certainty, reassurance, or that "just right" feeling. Compulsions and reassurance seeking may seem to alleviate your distress and offer short-term relief. So the next time you feel distressed by your thoughts, you're likely to use those strategies again because you've learned that they provide relief, even if it isn't long lasting. Doing nothing probably doesn't seem possible when your thoughts feel threatening, so you turn to compulsions again and again. Around and around you go, chasing certainty and trying to get rid of your obsessions and anxiety. Yet this puts you deeper in the grip of OCD because it strengthens the OCD cycle.

By her final semester in college, Mary's cleaning rituals had intensified. She told me, "I got up in the morning, and after cleaning the litter box and floors, I started scrubbing the toilet, the bathtub, and the bathroom sink. I scrubbed the kitchen floor and sink at the end of the day and after doing laundry, which I did every day. I washed whatever I wore that same day. More things start to bother me and compel me to wash."

Mary started showering at least twice every day—unless she encountered something that made her want to shower even more. She showered after being around anything that felt unclean to her: public transportation, public seats, items that looked old and dingy, or any unclean surface that might touch any part of her body. She washed her hands after touching a phone, someone else's pencil, or a doorknob.

Basically, she washed her hands after touching anything that someone else might have touched.

The more Mary engaged in cleaning compulsions, the more she cleaned when new situations triggered her anxiety. Here's her description of how her compulsions intensified:

> My friend Laura got food poisoning and threw up in my car, mostly on herself and only a tiny bit on the seat. When we got home, I grabbed some cleanser and headed out to the car. I cleaned the car seat several times. The next day after I took Laura to the airport, I came home and removed the fabric covers from the couch cushions where she had slept. I wanted to do this right away after she left, so I skipped class and called my boss and told him I was sick. I took the cover off each cushion, which was difficult because they were very tight. I took them all to the laundromat because my washer wasn't big enough. I scoured my car again and then took it to get detailed. I was sweating and exhausted from running back and forth from the laundromat. I got caught in that episode, and I was like a tornado, spinning around trying to get all the cleaning done. As I look back on it, it's hard to believe how automatically I went through the cleaning ritual and how much energy and time it took.

For Gina, although she tried to obtain certainty that harm wouldn't come to her family by engaging in tapping rituals and checking household appliances, new thoughts triggered anxiety and a further need for certainty. Here's how Gina explained it:

> When I was in the fifth grade, I was watching the movie *Cloak and Dagger* with my family. I remember feeling relief for the main character, a young boy, when he shot and killed the bad guys who were after him. Immediately, I felt disturbed that I was glad he had managed to kill the bad guys. How could I feel relief and happiness over the death of another human being? This started an endless cycle of questioning what I might be capable of. What-ifs flooded my mind: *What if I just picked up that knife*

and stabbed my mom? What if I drowned my sister? It was like a broken record playing in my head. Another time, as I sat in the chair next to my dad at the barbershop and watched the blade moving up and down his neck, I thought, *Would I slit my dad's throat if I were shaving him?* I tried to reassure myself that I wasn't capable of committing horrendous acts, but doubts intruded. I couldn't understand why those thoughts were so persistent. They disturbed me so deeply. Being around a knife, water, or anything that could potentially cause harm to someone paralyzed me with fear. My harming fears intensified, and I was held hostage by the need to perform compulsions.

Ted unknowingly worsened his OCD cycle by seeking reassurance and confessing anything he might possibly have done wrong. Although he was initially reassured, his relief was temporary. New doubts emerged, leading to more self-questioning and reassurance seeking and allowing the OCD cycle to take a stronger hold on him. Here's how Ted described his feelings on the day of his ordination as a priest:

While my classmates were just in heaven that day, I was in terror. If I didn't do the rituals right, I couldn't become a priest. There's actually not much you have to do, because the essential part of the ordination is the laying on of hands by the bishop, and that's pretty straightforward. He either lays his hands on your head or doesn't. But I had this big thing about intention, thinking, *Do I really want to be a priest?* As I performed the rituals, I questioned my actions: *Did I touch the paten with two fingers or just one?* I agonized over these questions in my head. By the end of the day I had a terrible migraine.

Of course, becoming ordained didn't stop Ted from engaging in the OCD cycle. As he performed his priestly duties and rituals, his doubts centered on themes of uncertainty, responsibility, and perfectionism. He sought certainty that he had done everything correctly. Officiating at baptisms, marriage ceremonies, and last rites led to endless doubts about performing perfectly. He feared being responsible for disastrous and even eternal consequences, thinking, *If the baptismal water didn't* touch the baby's forehead, she might not go to heaven. If witnesses didn't hear the "I dos" at weddings, couples might unknowingly live in sin. If I wasn't able to instill enough contrition in the dying and they had committed mortal sins, they could go to hell. Ted told me, "I didn't want to be responsible for a poor soul going to hell. If someone was comatose, I'd think to myself, Maybe I didn't try hard enough to make sure he could hear me. That thought always caused me so much anguish." Ted's battles with uncertainty and excessive responsibility were agonizing. He mentally reviewed services that he performed and checked with witnesses in search of certainty. Looking back on it, he said, "I think it was more about perfectionism than anything else."

You can see how Mary, Gina, and Ted got caught in the OCD cycle. Their attempts to relieve feelings of distress only worsened those feelings. The more importance they gave to their thoughts and the more they tried to "make things right" by engaging in rituals and searching for reassurance, the more they reinforced the importance of their thoughts, strengthening the OCD cycle.

Symptoms Morph: New Content, Same Cycle

Early OCD symptoms can be bothersome and time-consuming. As you got caught in the OCD cycle, your symptoms probably became more disturbing and started showing up more often. And to add to the complexity, symptoms often seem to morph. New obsessions emerge. New thoughts and situations trigger familiar feelings of distress. With new obsessions, new compulsions can develop. For example, an old obsession might involve uncertainty about whether you locked doors, prompting you to repeatedly check door locks; later, new doubts about the possibility of engaging in inappropriate sexual behaviors may trigger even more anxiety and lead to new behaviors, such avoiding standing near children or walking by playgrounds. Or an old obsession might involve being bothered by items not lining up "just right"; and then you begin to feel anxious when you don't know for sure that you understood what you read, so a rereading compulsion may join older compulsions to rearrange items that don't seem to be lined up perfectly. Alternatively, old compulsive behaviors may intensify to meet the demands of the new obsessions. Perhaps you developed a hand washing compulsion in response to feelings of disgust due to exposure to dirty things. Later, that compulsion may intensify because of a new obsession, such as feeling contaminated at the sight of people who somehow look like they may have been exposed to a communicable disease.

Although the content of your symptoms may change, it's important to remember that they're still linked to underlying OCD themes. The real problem in OCD is how you respond to underlying themes, no matter what form they take. In case you need a reminder, here are the main themes:

◆ Difficulty tolerating uncertainty

◆ Perfectionism or wanting things to be "just right"

◆ Having an inflated sense of responsibility and overestimating the probability and severity of threat

◆ Interpreting thoughts as overly important and believing it's important to control them

If your symptoms morphed, you may not have seen how the new symptoms make sense, given that they're also expressions of underlying OCD themes you might only gradually become aware of. Shifts in symptoms tend to be frightening, making it seem like more and more of your life is being consumed by fears and triggers. Yet the more you try to control your thoughts, the less in control you feel and the worse your symptoms become. You may feel like you're on a runaway train, with new triggers lurking around every corner. Yet the new manifestation of your problem isn't all that different, even though your symptoms may have changed.

Mary's contamination obsessions morphed into anxiety about images of anything that seemed unusual, unidentifiable, or disgusting:

My obsessive thoughts started to take the form of images— things I'd seen and couldn't shake from my mind. These images became threatening. I needed to wash after encountering anything I felt had contaminated me, even if it was something I had only heard about. It's hard to describe the feeling that precedes an urge to get rid of an image by washing. I didn't think I had been contaminated by something that had actually touched me. It was the thought that was contaminating, and it was the thought that I wanted to escape from. I constantly tried to disconnect from the images lodged in my head and I felt exhausted by the search for ways to not think about these images.

Mary always braced herself for what she might see when she left her house. She constantly wondered if someone or something would trigger her anxiety and urge to wash. She scanned her environment looking for, as she put it, alarms:

I call them alarms because that's how they feel: annoying, shrill thoughts that go in and don't come back out—triggered by a dirty floor, an odd-looking person serving coffee, or seeing something I couldn't identify with certainty. I walked out of hundreds of restaurants, coffee shops, and stores because something set off an alarm, like a criminal who hears an alarm bell, drops the money, and runs! There never was much consistency to my obsessive thoughts. It's one of the peculiarities of OCD; it doesn't always discriminate. The objects and places that bothered me changed over time. One ickiness got replaced by another ickiness. A new obsessive thought replaced an old one. The sight of a homeless woman with a diseased foot was replaced by the sight of a filthy restaurant bathroom. You can't escape images. Even when you shut your eyes, you still see them. With my new obsessions, image-based obsessions, the disturbing things I encountered became images stuck in my head. So I tried not to think about them. I tried to wash them off. I tried to figure them out. But what happened is that they attached themselves to me more and more.

Gina's symptoms morphed during her middle school years. She told me, "As if the harming fear wasn't enough, my OCD decided to give me another what-if when I was sitting in math class during junior high school. Another student walked by me, and I could smell her perfume. I thought it smelled really good, and immediately my mind said, *What if you're gay?* This triggered an onslaught of new doubts." Gina felt overwhelmed by doubts about her sexual orientation, and homosexual obsessions emerged. She looked for proof of whether she was gay or straight. She looked at pictures of both boys and girls to seek certainty about her feelings. She questioned every feeling, wondering *Is this feeling genuine or not?* She analyzed every thought and feeling she had about her friends. She knew that the intensity of her doubts didn't feel normal and noticed that the distress she felt from those thoughts was very similar to her harming fears.

Although Gina's doubts started to take on a new form, that didn't mean her harming doubts stopped. They just took a backseat when new doubts triggered her anxiety. So in addition to questioning the genuineness of every feeling she had about both women and men, she was still afraid to go home at night because she thought, *What if I slaughter my whole family?* As the content of her doubts flip-flopped, Gina prayed, *Please, God, let me have the sexual orientation fears instead. No, please God, let me have the harming fears back.* Whichever form her OCD took, she wished for the other one to replace it. And she was thankful when the other form was triggered, at least initially, because it gave her some relief from her current anxiety.

But there was more. Gina explained, "Entwined in these what-ifs was scrupulosity. I felt a need to always be morally right and to confess if I did something wrong. I was so confused about what was going on in my mind. I had no idea there was a name for the torment I was experiencing." Although the content of her obsessions changed, underlying OCD themes (intolerance of uncertainty and interpreting her thoughts as important) were at the heart of Gina's problem. Checking and reassurance seeking deepened her OCD cycle and spiraled into new themes.

As for Ted, during his last months in the priesthood he began dating a woman. Interestingly, at that time he wasn't plagued by scrupulosity; instead, he had intrusive thoughts about accidentally harming a pedestrian. Ted's obsessions shifted. Overestimation of new threats and his responsibility became more pronounced than his original scrupulosity obsessions. For example, after leaving the priesthood and marrying,

Ted repeatedly questioned whether he had closed the garage door due to concerns that intruders would rob him or possibly harm his wife. Ted told me, "Since these concerns typically came up while I was on my way to do something and I knew I'd return home soon, my rituals were internal. I usually freaked out and agonized about it for a while." Ted vividly recalls two other recurring obsessions from that time:

I used to walk by a place where a tree limb stuck out at a level that if someone was riding his bike on the sidewalk, the limb would hit him in the neck or face. I imagined serious if not fatal injury, especially if the cyclist was going at breakneck speed. I felt I should tell the residents of the house to cut the limb. But I also I felt that would be over-the-top, so I didn't do anything but agonize about it. I was also triggered by the thought of abandoned refrigerators after reading something in the newspaper about a child getting suffocated in one when his companions deserted him after closing the door. There were cautions in the media about taking the door off an abandoned fridge or springing the latch. My compulsion was to check whether that had been done on every abandoned fridge I saw. Abandoned refrigerators were hard to come by, yet I managed to find some and checked them out. I once called a city hotline to tell authorities about a fridge near a school when I didn't have the tools to take care of it myself. Anytime I didn't correct a possible danger, I was in anguish over what could happen and my irresponsibility for not doing anything about it.

During this phase, Ted struggled with many new obsessions. Thoughts about not detecting and reporting natural gas leaks or discarded slats of lumber with nails sticking out of them triggered countless hours of checking, mental checking, and reassurance seeking. His new obsessions led to repetitive questioning: *Could a street block be blown to smithereens because of a natural gas leak? Could someone get lockjaw and die after stepping on a rusty nail embedded in abandoned lumber? Will it be my fault for not detecting and reporting it?* Ted also had obsessive thoughts about stating opinions accurately. For example, he once told some friends, "I read in a health newsletter that there's nothing wrong with drinking coffee. In fact, they point out that it's beneficial in many ways." Later he had intrusive thoughts about the consequences of his words. Ted explained, "I worried that I should have given a caution about high blood pressure—that someone with high blood pressure would drink coffee and have a stroke, and it would be my fault. I agonized about that." Ted's symptoms eventually morphed into a combination of responsibility and contamination fears. For example, he worried about ant poison in his garage accidentally poisoning innocent people. Ted also told me that he had recently begun to notice frightening images that made him question whether he was capable of acting on them.

Mary, Gina, and Ted unwittingly reinforced the OCD cycle, and their symptoms intensified and morphed. They didn't know they were responding to underlying OCD themes. They reacted to triggers of intense anxiety and discomfort by using compulsions to alleviate their distress. When the urge to engage in compulsions arises, people usually aren't thinking about breaking the vicious cycle that spirals them into more distress. They want relief. They want unwanted thoughts, urges, and images—and the intense feelings of anxiety, disgust, or dread they elicit—to go away!

But when you use compulsions, you don't learn that you can tolerate the anxiety triggered by obsessions. The more you turn to rituals, seek reassurance, or avoid thoughts and situations, the more importance you give to the thoughts and images that frighten or disturb you. The more you follow your instincts to alleviate distress by whatever means you can, the more you strengthen the belief that you need to alleviate distress rather than ride it out.

As your symptoms intensify and morph, you might feel scared and alone. It may seem like your mind continually tries to find new ways to scare you. The idiosyncratic nature of your symptoms may cause you to think that your problem is one of a kind. After all, these are your thoughts and images, and your compulsions are personal and specific. You probably feel embarrassed by your thoughts and may even find them reprehensible. And to make matters worse, these thoughts don't go away! As new triggers pop up more often and your compulsions become harder to resist, it can seem as though there's no way out of the OCD cycle.

EXERCISE: Understanding Your OCD Cycle

Thinking about the progression of your symptoms will help you understand how you got caught in furthering the OCD cycle. This creates opportunities to see how to break the cycle now and respond to your obsessions differently. No matter how much your OCD symptoms may have changed over time, the underlying OCD themes continue to be in play. Using compulsions in response to the discomfort that they trigger only feeds the OCD cycle. In your journal, write your answers to the following questions, which will help you understand your own OCD cycle:

◆ How effective have compulsions and avoidance been in reducing your anxiety or distress? Do you find yourself using these strategies more frequently in response to obsessions? Have they made your symptoms worse over time? If so, how have they strengthened the OCD cycle?

◆ Have your symptoms changed or morphed? If so, how did they change? Did the content of your obsessions shift to new concerns? How would you describe the shift? Did new obsessions and situations lead to new compulsions or engaging in old compulsions more frequently?

◆ If your symptoms morphed and changed, do you recognize underlying OCD themes in your new obsessions? If so, what are those themes? Are your symptoms related to intolerance of uncertainty, wanting things to be perfect or "just right," overestimating threat or your responsibility, or interpreting thoughts as overly important and wanting to control them?

◆ When you think about breaking your OCD cycle by not using compulsions, how do you feel? What do you imagine when you think about learning to tolerate the anxiety and distress triggered by your obsessions rather than using compulsions? What concerns or fears do you have about starting treatment that aims to break the OCD cycle?

The Toll of Staying Stuck in the OCD Cycle

You know how exhausting and time-consuming it can be to deal with obsessions and engage in compulsions. In spite of repeated and sometimes extreme efforts, you find yourself back where you started or, even worse, more anxious and caught in new cycles of compulsions. And no matter how much you try to avoid triggering obsessions, triggers are everywhere. Potential contaminants and germs are everywhere. You can try to avoid people who you think might be contaminated, but inevitably you'll run into someone who triggers your fears. Opportunities to make mistakes are around every corner. Thoughts can pop into your head at any time, and the more you don't want to have a violent image or thought, the more it shows up, whether you're working at your desk, exercising at the gym, or walking by a park full of children playing. Questions about the genuineness of your intentions can trigger agonizing questions about your morals; you'll want answers to those questions, and you'll want to be certain about the answers. Reading magazine articles can trigger doubts about fully understanding everything you read. Writing a note can leave you stuck trying to write it perfectly. It can seem as though there's no way to escape triggering obsessions and compulsions.

Compulsions slow you down. Checking to be certain that you did something right can take minutes or hours. Paying bills can be an arduous task if you feel you have to repeatedly check to be sure you paid the right amount; all of that checking adds up. Making sure sentences line up just right on every page takes time away from other work or school assignments. Rereading to be certain you understood everything perfectly can cause you to spend hours reviewing articles or magazines that you weren't even interested in reading. These are just a few examples of how compulsions can slow you down and, more importantly, take time away from activities that you'd rather do.

Another unfortunate consequence of the OCD cycle is the toll it takes on the people around you. Loved ones face a huge dilemma if you ask them to comply with rituals that may reduce your anxiety in the short run but ultimately worsen your OCD symptoms. You may ask your children to wash their hands in a ritualized fashion. You may ask your spouse not to wear anything you deem to be contaminated. Loved ones may feel annoyed by requests to comply with what seem to be irrational rituals. They're likely to feel at wit's end if you repeatedly ask the same questions so you can once again try to obtain reassurance about whether something is dangerous or if you did everything "right." Sometimes these questions might be aimed at your loved ones; for example, "Are you certain that you were never exposed to an STD? Tell me again about your lovers' histories."

Ted tells a gripping story about how his checking behaviors led to unforeseen consequences many years ago when he was working in a small Mexican town as a priest. One day when he was performing a baptism, he thought, *I'm pretty sure I watched the water flow off the baby's head, but did I really see it? If I'm wrong, I'm going to hell because of my mortal sin. I'm not sure the water poured over the baby's forehead. It's all up in the air!* To relieve his doubts, he visited the baby's parents the next day to check whether they had seen the water flowing over the baby's forehead. When he told them that he might have to rebaptize their child, they told him that a rebaptism wasn't necessary. Ted told me, "The real reason was, of course, to relieve my doubt and anxiety, but I'm pretty sure they thought, *This Yankee priest is trying to perform another baptism to get another donation!*" The baby's family and neighbors were upset and angry. That night, someone set Ted's car on fire. He never intended to offend anyone, but his need to check was gravely misinterpreted.

Feeling at the mercy of the OCD cycle can mean avoiding friends, dates, intimacy, promotions, or educational opportunities. It can affect your future. As Mary became more entrenched in the OCD cycle, her friendships, romantic relationships, and career opportunities were jeopardized. After Gina had her first child and began to avoid being alone with her baby and giving her a bath, she realized that she was losing precious time and many opportunities to be the mother she wanted to be. And the more Ted checked in an attempt to obtain certainty, the more trouble he found. Feeding the OCD cycle can leave you feeling hopeless about living the life you want to live.

EXERCISE: Assessing the Toll of Your OCD Cycle

Seeing how your symptoms take a toll on your life, your loved ones, and your future can help you find the courage to break the OCD cycle. Assessing the costs is a challenging but important exercise. It can be difficult to confront the price you pay, but doing so can provide motivation to start getting the help you need. As you answer the following questions in your journal, be honest, but also be gentle with yourself:

◆ How does the OCD cycle affect your daily life? Does it cause you a lot of distress? Does it eat up a lot of your time? Does it take you away from activities that you'd rather do?

◆ How do your symptoms affect people in your life? Do your symptoms put a strain on your marriage or relationship? Do they prevent you from having an intimate relationship? Do they affect how you interact with your children? Do they affect how you interact with friends? Do you avoid people to avoid triggering an OCD episode? Do you involve others in your rituals?

◆ How does OCD affect your future prospects? Are you concerned about OCD interfering with your plans and hopes for the future? Do you worry that it may affect your career or job opportunities? Do you fear that it will take an increasing toll on your friendships, social life, and plans with your family?

Summary

Your intrusive thoughts and the ensuing compulsions once might have seemed merely odd, pesky, or annoying. But as you gave your thoughts greater importance, they probably intruded more frequently and seemed more threatening. Because compulsions gave you short-term relief from anxiety and distress, with time you probably turned to more compulsions for relief, doing so with a greater sense of urgency as your distress increased. This is the OCD cycle. And as the cycle strengthens, compulsions become increasingly disruptive and time-consuming. In addition, symptoms can morph and take on new forms.

You don't need to know exactly why you were vulnerable to developing OCD or exactly when your symptoms became a disorder to know how to treat it. What's most important is that you know how the OCD cycle works: how OCD is maintained and strengthened, and the role you play in perpetuating this cycle that causes so much distress. The OCD cycle will repeat itself until you intervene and change your responses when underlying themes and obsessions trigger the urge to engage in compulsions. In chapter 3, I'll discuss how treatment works and how to get started. Although you can't stop distressing thoughts, urges, and images from entering your mind, you can change how you think about and respond to them. However, as you probably know all too well, trying to break the cycle is hard to do alone. That's why it's important to get the help you need: to increase your chances of success and speed the process of breaking the OCD cycle and reclaiming your life.

CHAPTER 3

GETTING THE HELP YOU NEED

Because you're reading this book, you've probably decided that your symptoms are a problem. Hopefully you've decided that you want to break free from the OCD cycle. Doing so means facing distressing thoughts and emotions without engaging in compulsions. It sounds straightforward, and in a way, it is. The treatment rationale is clear: By changing your responses to distressing thoughts, you learn that you can handle the anxiety and discomfort they trigger. You change your expectations about the consequences of facing your fears. You learn that you can tolerate uncertainty, imperfection, and not feeling "just right." You learn that thoughts are just thoughts, and that having them doesn't mean you'll act on them. You learn that you don't need to use compulsions or avoid triggering disturbing thoughts and images.

The long-term gains from breaking the OCD cycle are great. Still, facing your fears isn't easy. If it was, you'd be doing it already! Maybe you already tried to break the OCD cycle on your own but became discouraged. Working with a therapist can help you make great strides.

Cognitive Behavioral Therapy for OCD

Cognitive behavioral therapy (CBT) is a type of therapy that encompasses a range of approaches and strategies shown to be effective for psychological problems. It's based on conceptualizing problems as resulting from problematic thoughts and behaviors. It has been studied extensively as a treatment for OCD and has been proven effective (Olatunji et al. 2013). When choosing a CBT therapist, find someone who's trained to provide CBT for OCD.

Exposure and response prevention, or ERP, is a CBT treatment approach considered to be the gold standard for treatment of OCD, and research supports its effectiveness (Abramowitz 1996; Franklin et al. 2000). The "exposure" part of ERP involves confronting your obsessions and the situations that trigger them. The "response prevention" part means not engaging in your usual responses, like using compulsions, and instead accepting your thoughts and feelings. Initially, your anxiety is likely to increase as you face your fears rather than avoid them, but if you stay with your feelings and don't try to escape from them, you'll learn that facing your fears doesn't result in the consequences you might expect. Of course, you'll never know this to be true unless you try it. That's the problem with the OCD cycle: in repeating the pattern of trying to escape and avoid uncomfortable feelings, you don't learn what happens if you allow yourself to feel discomfort. In ERP, instead of trying to escape discomfort, you intentionally face disturbing thoughts, urges, and images, and change your expectations about the consequences of doing so.

While ERP is the most common strategy used in OCD treatment, some CBT therapists focus on changing beliefs about intrusive thoughts by helping clients use a range of cognitive and behavioral strategies (Wilhelm and Steketee 2006). Cognitive approaches also incorporate *behavioral experiments*: strategies to help you challenge your beliefs by learning what happens if you don't use compulsions. For example, you can design experiments to test what happens if you think a "bad" thought about somebody, don't do something perfectly, or don't return home to check appliances. As in ERP, new learning occurs as you challenge your beliefs and change your responses to obsessive thoughts.

Acceptance and commitment therapy (ACT), one of a "new wave" of CBT approaches, helps you accept thoughts and feelings and take committed action toward life goals that are in line with your chosen values (Hayes 2005; Hayes, Strosahl, and Wilson 1999). Treatment helps you learn to *notice* and accept thoughts, emotions, and sensations rather than spending time and energy trying to fight or control them. When used to treat OCD, ACT aims to help you increase your willingness to experience obsessions and distressing emotions rather than avoiding discomfort by using compulsions and avoidance. ACT and ERP share many similarities (Arch and Craske 2008), including directly targeting behavioral change when used to treat OCD (Tolin 2009). Many clinicians combine components from ACT and ERP. These approaches can go hand in hand, since in order to change your behaviors and not respond to obsessions by using compulsions, it is important to be willing to have thoughts and feelings, including those that are uncomfortable and disturbing. Without willingness and commitment to behavioral change, you'll continue to seek short-term relief and try to escape discomfort. You won't be able to truly engage in response prevention.

All of these CBT approaches involve learning to think and respond differently when intrusive thoughts trigger feelings of distress. They help you break the OCD cycle by not engaging in avoidance or compulsions. Treatment teaches you how to practice new responses to obsessions, no matter what form they take. There's no way around it; you need to face your thoughts and the feelings they trigger rather than run from them.

Understanding Exposure and Response Prevention

Exposure is an effective treatment for most types of fear, not just those associated with OCD. For example, to overcome a spider phobia, you'd approach spiders, feel the anxiety that approaching them provokes, and learn that you can tolerate that anxiety without running away. You'd then become less fearful avoidant of spiders, not because spiders no longer trigger a fear response, but because you'd know that you can handle your anxiety and that your fears aren't likely to be realized. If you're afraid of public speaking because you fear embarrassment, treatment would involve facing your fears and learning that you can tolerate embarrassment and feelings of discomfort and still engage in public speaking. OCD involves fears of intrusive thoughts, urges, and images, and they can occur anywhere and at any time. ERP helps you face them rather than run from them and the feelings they provoke.

Exposure—intentionally facing situations that trigger distress—isn't necessarily time-consuming. For example, you might touch an item that feels contaminated, drive on a crowded street, tap an odd number of times rather than even, or read an article with disturbing content about people hurting their loved ones. Response prevention, on the other hand, often continues long after exposure to an OCD trigger. It involves not seeking reassurance, not decontaminating, not checking, not mentally reviewing, or not engaging in a host of other compulsions. It requires that you accept your thoughts and feelings, which may persist long after exposure to a trigger. For example, response prevention may mean accepting that you might be contaminated, that you might have committed an irresponsible act that will result in negative consequences for others, or that you could be capable of murder and will never know for sure. The exposure part—intentionally facing OCD triggers rather than avoiding them—is hard to do, but tolerating uncomfortable feelings and continuing to use response prevention when you're tempted to escape can feel much harder.

HOW ERP IS DIFFERENT FROM WHAT YOU DO NOW

You might think, *But I do confront thoughts and situations all the time, and my anxiety keeps getting worse!* It's likely that you engage in exposure, but then instead of using response prevention, you try to escape from feeling anxious. If you sit with discomfort, you'll learn that you can ride it out. You'll learn something that you never learn when you try to escape discomfort: that you can handle the uncomfortable feelings triggered by thoughts that seem threatening. And you'll change your expectations about what happens when you face your fears.

Mary found it helpful when her therapist told her stories to illustrate aspects of how ERP works and described two of the most helpful stories like this:

A scientist touches a sea slug and the slug has a startle response, but after several more touches, the slug stops responding. The slug realizes it's not being hurt by the touch. It's not really a threat. That's what happens in ERP. Before, I never gave myself the chance to learn that there was no real threat. Unlike the sea slug, I moved away from what I thought was threatening as quickly as I could. But my anxious response only increased the thought's hold on me. The more I tried to not feel anxious, the more my anxiety increased. That's the anxiety paradox. It's like a feedback loop: the more you try to get rid of anxiety, the more anxious you feel.

The signals that my brain sends when I see or hear something that triggers disgust or fear are a big overreaction—like I'm calling 911 for no real reason. It's like I'm experiencing an emergency when there isn't one. The smoke detector in my brain is too sensitive. It goes off when I'm making toast! My therapist explained that CBT would help me learn not to call 911. Instead, I'd learn to see my reactions as false alarms. I'd learn tools to help me not respond to faulty alarms. And eventually, the alarms wouldn't sound so often.

You may have already tried to practice ERP on your own by sitting with intrusive thoughts and not using compulsions. Most likely, you became overwhelmed by feelings of anxiety or thoughts about what could happen if you didn't use compulsions. You might even have tried to accept your thoughts and anxious feelings—until it became too tempting to look for ways to escape discomfort. In a subtle form of reassurance seeking, maybe you simply tried to convince yourself that everything was okay. Another problem you might have encountered was feeling confused about which thoughts and situations to face, when to face them, how to face them, and how to find time to face them. Obsessions can be triggered all day long. It can be hard to decide when to practice changing your responses to them, and taking on all of your OCD challenges at once would be overwhelming. As you tried to figure out when and how to try response prevention, your approach may have been haphazard, making it less effective. If you've felt overwhelmed and discouraged by previous efforts, working with a therapist to clarify the goals of ERP and plan an approach to facing your fears can make all the difference.

HOW TO PRACTICE ERP

To practice ERP, you make a list of situations and obsessions that trigger your distress, and you determine the feared consequences of your obsessive thoughts (for example: *I'll spread contamination and endanger others, I'll be responsible for disastrous consequences, I won't be able to tolerate feelings of discomfort,* or *I might act on my thoughts*). You also identify compulsions, such as hand washing, cleaning, checking, mental checking, repeating, "undoing," and reassurance seeking. Then you practice facing the situations and obsessions you've listed while tolerating discomfort instead of seeking relief through escape and avoidance.

ERP typically involves creating an exposure hierarchy by ranking situations and obsessions on your list from least stressful to most stressful and assigning each item a number on a scale from 0 (no discomfort) to 100 (maximum discomfort). This is called the *subjective units of discomfort scale* (SUDS). The long-standing practice of ERP has been to start with easier items before moving up to more difficult ones, based on the theory that you habituate to fears through repeated and prolonged exposure to them. Recent research has identified that a key component in exposure-based treatments is changing expectations about your fears (Craske et al. 2008). Exposure allows you to learn that your expectations about feared consequences of obsessions aren't accurate. Therefore, exposure sessions should continue until this new learning takes place. Applying the latest research on the importance of maximizing learning in exposure-based treatment to OCD, ERP is best practiced across different situations and may be most effective in the long term by staggering levels of difficulty rather than strictly adhering to a step-by-step hierarchy and only moving on to the next level after anxiety elicited by the current level has diminished (Abramowitz and Arch in press).

As you begin treatment, you'll probably work with your therapist to break down exposure exercises into smaller steps. For example, if touching all public doorknobs without washing your hands in a ritualized fashion feels too difficult, you may start with doorknobs that seem less contaminated before practicing with those that seem more contaminated. Or you may start by decreasing the length of time or number of times that you wash your hands, rather than forgoing hand washing altogether. You'll work with your therapist to decide which exposures to start with and which responses you'll change. The goal is to change your expectations about what will happen when you face your fears.

Whenever possible, ERP is practiced using situations that you can face in the here and now, like touching doorknobs and not washing your hands, or refraining from returning home to do checking rituals. However, some situations can't be faced in the here and now. For example, you may have fears that loved ones will die because of actions you took many years ago, or you may fear that having a thought about killing your spouse means that you will actually do it someday. To practice ERP with these kinds of thoughts, you can create *imaginal exposures*, personalized scripts of scenarios that you create in your imagination. Just as with real-life practices, the goal is to face thoughts and images without using compulsions to avoid or decrease the distress they may cause.

Levels of Treatment

Treatment for OCD typically involves meeting with a therapist one to three times per week, allowing enough time to practice ERP in session and plan homework for between sessions. Frequent sessions early on can help jump-start your treatment, with the frequency and length of sessions tapering off as treatment progresses and the focus shifts to relapse prevention goals. For treatment to be successful, you must commit to doing ERP homework, which can be quite time-consuming.

When people suffer from severe symptoms that greatly interfere with their functioning or when their symptoms feel so overwhelming that it's too difficult to commit to practicing homework between sessions, participating in an intensive treatment program offering daily sessions, often many hours long, is a treatment option to consider. You may find such a program close to home or you may need to travel some distance to attend one. After completing an intensive program, you might resume or begin meeting with a therapist close to home once or twice a week, with a focus on goals such as continuing ERP practices, maintaining progress, and preventing relapse. Inpatient programs specializing in OCD treatment can be extremely beneficial for people suffering from especially severe symptoms. When you meet with a therapist who specializes in treating OCD, you can discuss which treatment options best fit your needs and circumstances. If you already think intensive treatment may be what you need, you can contact clinics directly to discuss arranging a consultation. The website of the International OCD Foundation (see Resources) provides a list of clinics and programs that offer intensive treatment options.

The Role of Medication

Another effective treatment for OCD involves medications called selective serotonin reuptake inhibitors (SSRIs) and a serotonin reuptake inhibitor (SRI) called clomipramine. Medication, ERP, and the two combined have all been shown to be effective for treating OCD, though combining medication with ERP doesn't necessarily make ERP more effective. Some people will benefit from a combined approach using ERP and medication, especially when symptoms are severe, other symptoms are present, or it's difficult to engage in ERP. Although some people prefer not to take medications due to side effects, they can be a lifesaver if you suffer from severe symptoms or have concurrent problems, such as depression. If you're thinking about taking medication without CBT, you should consider that gains made while taking medications are not likely to be sustained if medication is discontinued.

When you meet with your therapist, you can discuss whether or not medication seems like a good option for you. If you decide it would be helpful, consult with a psychiatrist who's knowledgeable about medication options for treating OCD. Then, as you practice new behavioral responses to the anxiety and distress triggered by obsessions, you'll probably be able to successfully discontinue the medication and rely instead on your new skills. For example, Mary chose to take an SSRI when she began treatment but successfully discontinued it as she practiced ERP. Gina chose not to take medication due to potential side effects, while Ted didn't feel medications were necessary for him.

Family Involvement

OCD doesn't occur in isolation. Your OCD affects your family members, and your family members can affect your symptoms, mood, and treatment. When you suffer from the distress caused by obsessions and engage in compulsions or avoidance, those around you are affected too. As discussed in chapter 2, your OCD symptoms can take a toll on your loved ones. At the same time, how your loved ones respond to your OCD symptoms can take a toll on you. For example, they might be critical of you for engaging in compulsions, become angry when you seek reassurance, or intentionally trigger your obsessions because they want to show you that your fears are unfounded.

Alternatively, if your loved ones are supportive and understand your symptoms and treatment, this can greatly enhance treatment effectiveness. Involving your spouse or significant other throughout the course of treatment can be helpful in achieving your treatment goals and can also help remedy relationship problems, including those related to OCD symptoms (Abramowitz et al. 2013). It's worth considering and discussing with your therapist how to include your significant other not only in supporting your treatment but also in playing a role that contributes to your recovery.

Getting Started

You may hesitate to call and initiate treatment, or you may feel so tired of dealing with OCD that you're ready to take the leap and get started. Most clients call me to discuss treatment only after their symptoms become too extreme to ignore. But there's no need to wait until your symptoms are severe to seek treatment.

Sometimes the "creep-up factor" delays people in getting the help they need. The OCD cycle may have become a familiar part of your life, making it difficult to decide when to seek treatment. Mary eventually realized that something was terribly wrong, but the "creep-up factor" blurred her ability to see that she had a problem earlier. By the time she sought treatment, her symptoms were severe:

> OCD incidents began colliding and running into each other. They weren't spaced out anymore. They became so frequent that I got confused about which obsession was bothering me more! I thought that this must be what it feels like to go crazy: having too many disturbing thoughts in my head at once. I tried to push them all out. I tried to figure them out. I tried not to have them: images from disgusting bathrooms, overflowing litter boxes, a face covered with acne. The disturbing movie of OCD images played continuously. Intrusive thoughts were getting in the way of enjoying anything in my life.

At that point, Mary finally realized it was time to get treatment. After researching her symptoms and treatment options, she called a local university clinic.

Some people delay treatment simply because they don't realize that they have a known disorder and that effective treatment is available. This was the case for Gina, who suffered during her childhood, adolescence, and early adulthood, fearing the worst about what her thoughts meant about her:

> Having these thoughts and not knowing that I wasn't alone caused me great distress and confusion. I believed that one day I'd end up in a straitjacket in a mental institution. I truly believed this was a real possibility. I recall crying one time as I stood staring at my face in a mirror and wondering how this could be the face of a killer. The hardest part in all of this was not having anyone to share these thoughts with out of fear of what others might think of me. On a couple of occasions I tried to share with my mom, but how do you tell your own mother that you've had thoughts of stabbing her in the belly? I loved my family. Why would I have these thoughts?

Gina hid her symptoms as long she could, and due to the nature of her OCD, this was fairly easy to do. Disturbing aggressive and sexual thoughts aren't visible to others. Mental checking and reassurance seeking may not be obvious. And if you've spent years feeling alone, internally tormented and attempting to hide your symptoms, calling a professional to seek help can be terrifying. You may worry about what will happen if others find out that you agonize about whether you could be a murderer or child molester. You may also worry about what a therapist might think of you, but therapists specializing in treating OCD will understand your symptoms.

Gina turned a corner just a couple of weeks prior to getting married. She had been questioning how she could ever know for sure that her feelings for her fiancé were genuine. She wanted her doubting thoughts to leave her alone and pleaded, *Make it stop!* Then, while watching a TV talk show, she learned that her thoughts and fears had a name: OCD. She searched online to learn about OCD and was relieved to finally understand her symptoms:

> When I finally learned that there was a name for what I was going through and that I wasn't alone, I felt as if God reached down and removed this huge boulder off of my shoulders. To finally know that you aren't insane is a relief I can't put into words. I felt so light at that moment that I knew I could finally share with my mom. She immediately found a psychologist for me to see. It was time to start treatment.

Ted, on the other hand, wasn't reticent about seeking treatment. He spent many years trying to find a therapist who could help him. He persistently consulted with psychiatrists and therapists hoping to find answers to his problem. For decades, therapists didn't understand how to treat his symptoms:

> I saw a succession of therapists who were unaware of OCD or how to treat it. Eventually, each would get to the point where they would say, 'Well, you're managing just fine,' as if they had helped me get to that point. With each therapist, I hoped that I

had found someone who could really help, but then I ran the same gamut. What finally helped was getting a diagnosis and learning about OCD, but that didn't happen until fifteen or sixteen years ago.

Upon learning that he had OCD, Ted immediately joined an OCD support group, where he learned about ERP. Finally, he'd found a treatment that could help him. He couldn't wait to get started.

Starting Treatment Can Feel Scary!

Ted's story may not necessarily be yours. Once you know what's involved in ERP, you might feel apprehensive about getting started. Most of my clients with OCD have told me that even though their symptoms wreaked havoc on their lives, it was still hard to make the call to initiate treatment. OCD may feel horrible, but at least it's familiar. Beginning treatment raises a host of unknowns. You may have reservations about starting treatment because you don't know what to expect. You may prefer to try to manage your OCD symptoms rather than face your fears head-on in therapy. ERP can sound scary! Here's how Mary described her thoughts before starting treatment. Perhaps you have similar fears:

I had no idea what to expect when I made my first appointment. I had reservations about CBT and wondered, *What is it? How does it work? Will it work?* The truth is, I had very little hope that anything would work for my OCD or whatever this thing that I did in my mind was. When I thought about CBT, I could only imagine a barnyard—a barnyard I had seen in a film where a group of people with OCD all took a field trip. In the van on the way to the barnyard, the group leader gets up and, like a drill sergeant, demands, "Give up your wet wipes!" One by one the passengers reluctantly take out packages of sanitizing wipes and drop them in a paper bag. I remember thinking that it must seem quite funny to normal people, but it made me uncomfortable.

When the OCD group arrives at the farm, the woman leads them into a large, fenced-in muddy area. They all get down on their knees and stick both hands into the mud—and whatever else was in the mud—and rub their hands together in the mud for five minutes. The leader times it. At the end of a very dramatically portrayed five minutes, all of them run toward a large trough of water with a spigot and start washing. They end up having fun throwing the water all over the place, spraying each other and laughing. The next stop was to feed the animals. One of the older men gets shat on by a cow. It gets all over him, and again, the rest of them are all laughing. So when I thought about CBT, I thought about the barnyard. I thought about putting my fists into mud and animal poo.

In Gina's case, she was relieved to learn that help was available to treat her symptoms, but she had concerns:

I didn't want to tell a psychologist about my fears about being gay because I hadn't heard of sexual orientation obsessions and was sure he would just say I was gay. I couldn't hear that. I loved my fiancé and was attracted to him. I was reluctant to start treatment because I feared I might learn that I didn't have OCD or that this treatment wasn't going to work for me. What if my fears were real and CBT couldn't help me? That wasn't the reality I wanted. If I didn't go to a therapist, there would always be a chance that my fears were just OCD.

Like Gina, you may feel hesitant about meeting with a therapist because you fear being told that your symptoms aren't OCD. This is especially true for people who have unwanted aggressive or sexual thoughts. If you've been living in fear of your thoughts, terrified that they mean you could be capable of committing murder or engaging in inappropriate sexual behavior, it can feel particularly terrifying to tell someone about your thoughts and fears. You may wonder, *What if a therapist confirms my worst fears and tells me that I'm a dangerous person? Will a therapist call the authorities when I share my scary and awful thoughts?*

Not all therapists understand how to differentiate OCD symptoms from other problems, but those trained in treating OCD do. They understand the nature of distressing unwanted thoughts. Of course, feelings of shame or embarrassment may still make it hard for you to contact a mental health professional, but if you find an OCD specialist, you'll be contacting someone who understands your problem and has heard it before.

EXERCISE: Weighing the Advantages and Disadvantages of Committing to Treatment

You may feel hesitant about committing to treatment. This exercise will help you clarify compelling advantages to committing to treatment and identify concerns that might be obstacles to getting started. Later, you can discuss your list with a therapist and brainstorm solutions for overcoming the obstacles you identify. Looking at costs and benefits is a tried-and-true strategy that you probably already use before committing to many important decisions. It's a helpful way to address ambivalence about making changes, including deciding whether to embark upon treatment.

In your journal, divide two pages into two columns. On the first page, write the heading "Commit to treatment and learn to face my fears without using compulsions." On the second, write the heading "Don't commit to treatment and continue using compulsions to cope with my fears." Then, on each page, list as many of the advantages and disadvantages to each as you can. Here's an example of an Advantages and Disadvantages Worksheet filled out by Sue, a married professional woman with a young child, whose OCD symptoms are affecting her marriage, her daughter, and her work.

Sue's Advantages and Disadvantages Worksheet

Option: Commit to treatment and learn to face my fears without using compulsions.

Advantages	Disadvantages
I might get better.	I'll have to take risks that don't feel right.
I'll be a good role model for my daughter.	It will feel really scary.
My relationship with my husband will be better.	I'll probably feel worse before I feel better.
I'll free up time to do other things.	Treatment will take time and energy.
I'll feel better about myself for trying.	Treatment is expensive.
I'll be in charge of my life, not OCD!	It might not work. Maybe I can't do it.

Option: Don't commit to treatment and continue using compulsions to cope with my fears.

Advantages	Disadvantages
I still get some immediate relief.	I don't get better; my OCD gets worse.
I avoid risking bad outcomes; it feels safer.	My life gets more limited and restricted.
Therapy might not work, and then I'll lose hope.	I get anxious about more and more things.
I've done it for so long; it's familiar.	My daughter is starting to notice and ask me why I do these things.
Therapy is expensive.	I'm restricting my daughter's activities.
	My husband can't take much more of this.
	I can't hide this at work much more. People are noticing my behaviors.
	Because of my rituals, it takes so long to get anything done. It's time-consuming.
	It's harder to enjoy myself when I go places.
	I have to avoid more and more people now, even some good friends.
	It's embarrassing when people see me do these odd things.

After completing your lists of advantages and disadvantages, consider the following questions and write your responses in your journal:

- ◆ Do some of the advantages and disadvantages listed by Sue sound familiar to you? Did you write down other thoughts?

- ◆ When you put together all of the advantages and disadvantages of committing to treatment or not, what do you conclude?

- ◆ Are any items deal breakers for you, meaning they prevent you from wanting to commit to treatment? If so, can you identify specific fears that talking to a therapist might help you resolve?

- ◆ Are any of the things you listed especially compelling in terms of making it worthwhile to commit to treatment?

Finding the Right Therapist

If you decide to pursue treatment, be sure to find a therapist who knows how to treat OCD. Fortunately, there are many skilled CBT therapists who specialize in treating OCD and some good resources for finding them. If you work with a therapist who isn't trained to treat OCD, you may waste valuable time and money and not receive the help you need. If a potential therapist or psychiatrist doesn't understand treatment for OCD, continue your search until you find one who does.

Ted's story indicates how important it is to be well educated about OCD. He was eager to learn everything he could about OCD and started at an OCD support group, which pointed him to the website for the International OCD Foundation:

What I read was a revelation to me and gave me new hope. I read every possible article about ERP. I remember finding a link to all of the articles Dr. Fred Penzel had written about various forms of OCD. I read them all. I called about six therapists on my health plan's list, but none of them knew about ERP. I wanted to start ERP as soon as possible, and I decided to find an ERP therapist even if I had to pay the full fee.

Following suggestions from his OCD support group, Ted found a CBT provider with expertise in ERP. He filed a grievance with his HMO after his search for such a therapist within his health plan was unsuccessful, and he received reimbursement for some of his sessions. Ted was enthusiastic about starting treatment and began preparing for ERP before he even met with his therapist.

Gina also had difficulty finding a qualified therapist. The first provider she visited wasn't even familiar with OCD. She told me, "The doctor had to look up OCD in a book! I never went back." Although discouraged, Gina continued to look for a CBT therapist with expertise in treating OCD. Her insurance company gave her the names of forty CBT therapists on their panel. She told me, "Not one of them was qualified to treat OCD. I asked direct questions, such as 'How do you treat OCD?' and 'How would you handle this problem?' If they were baffled, I knew they couldn't help me. And I knew that if I was in the wrong hands, my OCD might get worse. I knew I needed to find someone with expertise." None of the providers on Gina's insurance panel could help her. Through the help of an online support group, Gina eventually found the right therapist, but insurance didn't cover her treatment.

You may have had similar experiences in learning about OCD and mustering the courage to seek help. Unfortunately, not all treatment providers are knowledgeable about treatment for OCD, and not all OCD treatment providers are on insurance panels. It can be a frustrating process, but finding the right help makes all the difference in gaining the upper hand on OCD. For organizations that can help you find CBT therapists who treat OCD, see the Resources section at the back of this book. Contacting CBT therapists in your area can also be a good start, but be sure to ask whether they have training and experience in treating OCD and whether they're familiar with ERP. Sometimes it may take a few consultation sessions and referrals to find a potential therapist, but it's worth it if it leads you to the right one. Hopefully, with more OCD resources and therapists trained to treat OCD available these days, your search for the right therapist will be fairly straightforward.

Meeting Your Therapist

You might feel nervous about going to your first CBT consultation session, and question whether this therapist will be the right person to help you. You might feel hopeful about treatment but wonder if the therapist will understand your symptoms and what you've been through. Fortunately, if you've found a CBT therapist specializing in OCD, chances are your first meeting will allay those concerns. Here's how Mary described her impressions when she first met her therapist:

His office was quite the opposite of the barnyard scene I had imagined. It was warm and cozy. As I told him about several recent OCD episodes, he nodded as if he'd heard it before. It didn't faze him. And he didn't have that look. You know the one: you tell someone about your OCD and they appear worried and disturbed. He just listened and nodded. His nodding was a big deal to me. I held the common belief that my OCD was my own personal form of screwed-up thinking, so one of a kind. His nodding told me that it wasn't. I'd read plenty of educational material about OCD, but books and articles can't nod back at you.

As I sat with my therapist during our first session, I wondered if he had OCD. He was warm and understanding. He was nonchalant when talking about OCD, and his manner was comforting. How can someone who doesn't have OCD really get it? How can they know how to help? I hear many people in my OCD support group talk about this concern when starting therapy. Ironically, obsessive-compulsives spend their lives trying to run from their OCD and very little time trying to figure it out. CBT therapists, on the other hand, spend their lives figuring it out so they can treat it. It's hard to believe that someone who doesn't have OCD can understand what you're going through. So I asked him. He said that he didn't have OCD but that he understood the problem and had treated many other people with OCD. He sounded so confident. I could tell that he really got me. That's huge. I trusted him. He understood OCD, and I felt it as he listened to me recount my OCD episodes.

When Gina met her first CBT therapist with expertise in treating OCD, she found him to be a soft-spoken grandfatherly figure. She liked and trusted him right away:

He was warm and welcoming, and he was knowledgeable about OCD. He took me seriously, and I could tell that he genuinely cared. He knew I was worried that my symptoms might not be OCD. He said, "I'll tell you this one time and you'll never hear me say it again: You have OCD." Later I came to realize why he emphasized that he would only tell me once. Reassurance makes OCD worse. But at that time I needed to hear that I wasn't crazy. He shared stories of what OCD symptoms look like, and I knew he got it. He had heard it all before. He didn't call the police. His understanding that this was a disorder and that I wasn't a bad person helped me lower my guard. I knew that I could trust him and that he didn't think I was crazy.

By the time Ted met a CBT therapist who understood how to treat his symptoms, he was more than ready to start treatment. He didn't have many questions. Because he'd spent so much time researching ERP, he went to his first CBT session prepared with a list of situations and thoughts to use in an ERP hierarchy, which you'll find below. (Recall that the term SUDS, which appears in the hierarchy, stands for *subjective units of discomfort*.) Ted told me, "My therapist was surprised to see how much I had already done in preparation for treatment. She marveled at what I already knew about OCD and ERP. I had created my list of distressing situations and had rated them. I really wanted to make this work!" Ted finally had full confidence in a therapist, and he felt that his therapist had full confidence in him.

Ted's Initial Hierarchy

Situation	SUDS
Water not touching the baby's forehead during the baptism in Mexico	20
Missing broken glass on a sidewalk or in the park	40
Not knowing for certain if I might be gay	50
Being a fraud (maybe my BA degree isn't official?)	60
Making a misstatement that causes harm, like saying coffee can be beneficial	75
Not reporting a dangerous limb on tree, so it causes an accident and harms a bicyclist	80
Missing an abandoned refrigerator, resulting in harm to a child	85
Missing a gas leakage and nails protruding from lumber	90
Neighbors being contaminated by my ant poison	95
Planes crashing because I didn't make a report	100

Planning Treatment

Prior to treatment, Mary and Gina educated themselves about CBT for OCD, but unlike Ted they went to their initial sessions without fully understanding the nuts and bolts of what they would be expected to do in treatment. In your initial sessions with a CBT therapist, you'll learn about treatment for OCD and discuss a treatment plan designed specifically for you. Here's how Mary described what she thought as she learned about ERP and what treatment would involve:

My therapist introduced the idea of exposure to thoughts and images and feeling the anxiety by staying with thoughts and images instead of avoiding them. Instant fear set in—flashback of the barnyard in the film! I pictured myself standing there waiting to put my hands in the poo. I thought about lying to him.

If I didn't tell him all my fears, I wouldn't have to expose myself to them. Just the word "exposure" sent chills up my spine. I'd heard of exposure therapy and had an inkling about what it involved, but I was so terrified of the idea that I'd never found out much about it. I shut my ears! Of course I imagined the worst: sitting in a gas station bathroom for hours on end, licking a pole, eating bugs—weird reality TV–type stuff. Needless to say, I was bracing myself for my therapist's ideas about exposure.

When I asked him what kinds of things I'd have to do to feel the anxiety, he assured me that we wouldn't be going on any field trips to farms. We would work together to decide on exposure practices and homework that would be most effective for my OCD. At the mention of homework, I once again thought I might have to lie. What would I have to do? How would he know if I actually did it? Would I be able to tell my boyfriend about my homework? Would I be doing things at home?

Mary's concerns and questions are common. It's normal to have concerns before getting started. It makes sense that you might hesitate to tell your therapist about everything you avoid when you know that treatment involves facing your OCD-related fears instead of avoiding them. Practicing ERP for homework may sound daunting. Thinking about ERP can feel scary enough; planning your specific practices can feel even more frightening since, when you make a treatment plan with your therapist, ERP starts to feel much more real. Your therapist might offer some examples of initial ERP practices that you can discuss together. For example, Mary learned that she could begin by practicing holding a certain image in her mind. She could also begin by trying to change her washing rituals rather than eliminating them altogether. Mary found it comforting that she wouldn't be told to do anything; her therapist would suggest homework practices, and she would play an active role in choosing what to practice.

Gina felt relieved when her therapist confirmed that she had OCD, and she was comforted by her therapist's warm and understanding demeanor. Yet the idea of fully accepting her feared thoughts and images seemed difficult and out of reach. When her therapist explained what specific ERP practices for her doubts might look like, such as looking at women in *Playboy* magazine or putting a gay pride sticker on her car, her initial reaction was *No way!* As she told me, "My therapist explained what ERP was and how it worked. He explained it in a way that made sense, but I was scared to death of it, thinking, *What if it doesn't work? That could mean that I'm gay and shouldn't be married to my husband. Maybe I could be capable of murder. Maybe it's better to just not know!*" Gina signed on for treatment but was ambivalent about committing to many ERP exercises.

Gina's reaction is also common. People usually understand the rationale for ERP and feel ready to give it a try, but it can be hard to commit to specific and frightening ERP practices. Remember, you'll work with your therapist to choose ERP practices, and you can start with those that feel more manageable. Once you experience how ERP works, you'll be in a better position to fully commit to harder practices. It also isn't unusual to have fears and concerns about treatment not working. You may worry that, instead, your worst fears will be realized. Of course, that's why you engage in compulsions: you want to feel reassured, and avoid disturbing thoughts or images. If you're concerned that ERP practices will be too difficult, I encourage you to think about your alternatives. You can continue to do what you're doing now, which only causes you to suffer. Or you can take a risk and commit to treatment.

EXERCISE: Preparing for Treatment

Do you think it's possible for you to make strides in breaking the OCD cycle with the assistance of a therapist? Write down your thoughts and feelings in regard to treatment in your journal. Consider whether you may want some additional support. Are there people you can ask for help and support as you begin treatment? Do you think you might need to pursue more intensive treatment at first? Make notes about what you think you might need.

Also make some notes about what you want to look for in a therapist, based on what you've learned in this chapter. Think about what you want to know before you start treatment, and write down any questions you want to ask when you call or meet with potential therapists.

Summary

Treatment for OCD takes aim at breaking the OCD cycle. Cognitive behavioral therapy is an evidence-based treatment that will help you face obsessions and the situations that trigger them without seeking relief through compulsions or avoidance. ERP is the gold standard of treatment for OCD. It involves intentionally facing intrusive thoughts, urges, or images and allowing yourself to feel discomfort rather than resorting to compulsions. You learn what you can't learn when you engage in compulsions or try to avoid distress: that you can tolerate your feelings, however uncomfortable they may seem. You change your expectations about what will happen when you face your fears and learn that you don't need to live your life at the mercy of compulsions and avoidance.

You may have fears about starting treatment, but with the help of a therapist trained in treating OCD, you'll collaboratively decide where to begin and at what pace you'll proceed. Treatment isn't effortless, but it may not be as frightening as you imagine. And even if the prospect is frightening, it's well worth doing. In chapter 4, I'll discuss why.

CHAPTER 4

WHY TREATMENT IS WORTH IT

Learning about treatment for OCD can scare people away before they even start. You've learned that compulsions don't work and, in fact, make your problem worse by perpetuating the OCD cycle. You understand the basics of treatment and how ERP works. Yet ERP involves facing your fears, and that can be a hard step to take. In this chapter, I discuss why it's a step that's well worth taking and answer questions that clients often ask—questions you may also have.

Deciding whether to commit to treatment is a pivotal moment. I tell my clients that my job is easy; they are the ones who will need to do the hard work. The therapist's job is to explain, guide, and support people through the treatment process. For treatment to be effective, you need to fully engage in exposures and refrain from using compulsions. You need practice between sessions as well as during sessions.

You may be thinking, *Why should I do this? Is it worth it?* It may be that your family and friends are hoping you'll start treatment, while you yourself are not so sure it's something you want to do. Thinking about the toll of OCD and considering the advantages and disadvantages of committing to treatment may help you decide it's worth it but you might still be nervous and concerned about what you're committing to. You might wonder, *What will my therapist ask me to do?* It's important to remember that treatment will be a collaborative process between you and your therapist. Your therapist will guide you and encourage you to take on some hard challenges, but only you can decide whether you'll do them.

You're the one who must choose whether or not to embark on this journey. You'll be the one facing your fears, and doing so takes a lot of courage. People who don't understand OCD may not understand how hard this is. But your therapist will understand and appreciate how much courage it takes to do ERP. Those who have OCD will get it. People who have done ERP can tell you why it was worth it for them.

Still, you may remain ambivalent about whether the challenges of ERP are worth it for you. I find that certain concerns tend to come up for many new clients. Since you may have similar concerns, this chapter is devoted to answering some of the questions I hear most frequently:

◆ *How can I know for sure that treatment will work?*

◆ *Why can't I just leave things as they are?*

◆ *If I know my fears are OCD, why bother doing ERP?*

◆ *What if exposure practices make my OCD worse?*

◆ *What if I'm not careful enough and something bad does happen?*

◆ *If I face my fears, won't new ones pop up?*

◆ *Can't I get better some other way?*

If these questions sound familiar, you're not alone. I hear them a lot. It's helpful to address these concerns so you'll understand treatment and feel ready to commit to it.

"How Can I Know for Sure That Treatment Will Work?"

The truth is, you can't know for sure that treatment will work. CBT is an effective treatment for many people with OCD, so there's a good chance that it will be effective for you. Yet the desire for certainty is an integral part of OCD, and it may impact your decision making about treatment. Remember, intolerance of uncertainty is a core theme that underlies OCD. However, it's unrealistic to expect 100 percent certainty about almost anything in life, including treatment outcomes. In fact, by deciding to start treatment, you'll be taking a giant step toward breaking free from the grip of OCD. You'll be challenging the need for certainty by taking a chance on treatment.

Still, you may wonder, *Is it worth the risk?* Gina did. She worried that CBT might not work for her or that her worst fears might be true. The clearer you are about why you're willing to face your fears, the easier it will be to do it. In chapter 3 you listed advantages and disadvantages of committing to ERP and learning to tolerate discomfort and anxiety rather than engaging in compulsions. Reviewing that exercise and discussing it with a therapist or with supportive family members and friends can help you decide it's worth it. One of the most compelling disadvantages you may have listed is the prospect, if you commit to treatment, of facing the anxiety and distress that go with accepting uncertainty. Giving up the goal of seeking certainty and immediate relief is hard to do, but when you look at the disadvantages of engaging in compulsions, you can see that striving to obtain certainty doesn't work very well. In fact, it makes OCD worse.

Why Taking a Chance on Treatment Is Worth It

Looking at the advantages of treatment in the long term will help you clarify why you're willing to experience short-term discomfort and take risks. It will be helpful to remember the big picture and the advantages to taking a risk by committing to treatment in the face of fears that it won't work. You have a lot to gain.

"Why Can't I Just Leave Things As They Are?"

You may prefer to leave things the way they are rather than face the discomfort of ERP. If your hesitation stems from the fear of facing anxiety and discomfort, I encourage you to consider an especially important disadvantage of leaving things as they are: if you strengthen the OCD cycle by using compulsions or avoidance to achieve short-term relief from discomfort, your problems will probably worsen.

Let's revisit the OCD cycle to see why this is the case: When you have an intrusive thought, often triggered by something that you see or hear, and the thought seems threatening, you become highly anxious or uncomfortable. You focus excessively on your fears. To reduce anxiety and discomfort, you give in to compulsions, which may provide some immediate or short-term relief. Then you probably go out of your way to avoid triggering dreaded thoughts (and the associated perceived risks) again. Nevertheless, intrusive, frightening thoughts and the triggers for those thoughts are bound to arise again. And because you've reinforced the behavior of using compulsions or avoidance many times before, you'll probably continue to do so again and again.

Compulsions and avoidance strengthen the belief that anxiety or discomfort is too overwhelming to handle, and that if you hadn't used compulsions or avoided triggers your catastrophic fears might have been realized. In efforts to avoid triggers, you can change your route to work, move out of your apartment, quit a job, or even avoid activities with family and friends, but obsessions can be triggered anywhere and at any time. Mary, Gina, and Ted tried to avoid triggering their obsessions, but as you saw, their problems only intensified. Many of my clients sought treatment only after their lives became consumed by compulsions and efforts to avoid triggering obsessions. They were living with almost constant anticipatory anxiety about triggering more obsessions. Yet in spite of being masters of avoidance, they found that they couldn't escape their obsessions after all.

Unfortunately, unless the OCD cycle is interrupted, it only grows stronger. If new thoughts scare you or new situations trigger intrusive thoughts, you're likely to respond by using more compulsions. If new places, people, or objects trigger frightening intrusive thoughts and you try to avoid them, you'll find yourself avoiding more and more of your life. The more you engage in compulsions and avoidance, the more likely you are to use the same strategies when you encounter new triggers. OCD truly becomes a vicious cycle from which there is no escape other than to change your responses. In chapter 2, you saw how the OCD cycle worsened over time for Mary, Gina, and Ted. Now let's take a closer look. Tanya's story is a good example of how compulsions can seem relatively harmless at first but will grow and intensify if the OCD cycle isn't broken.

Tanya: Why It Doesn't Work to Leave Things as They Are

Before leaving her house, Tanya checks to be sure that the refrigerator door is closed, faucets aren't dripping, small appliances are unplugged, and the stove is turned off. She has a ritual of counting to ten while she stares at each item to be sure it is as it should be. She repeats the ritual several times before leaving the house. If she doubts whether she checked properly, she repeats the entire ritual. She repeatedly checks the front and back door locks to be sure they're bolted. She wants certainty that she didn't leave anything unlocked, plugged in, or turned on. Checking takes twenty minutes each morning, but Tanya allows for the extra time so she can complete her morning routine. She dreads her morning rituals, but dreads the prospect of not completing them even more. She decides that these behaviors ultimately don't interfere with her life very much. She engages in rituals in her work as a store manager too, but she avoids the most frightening trigger of her responsibility and uncertainty themes by making sure she isn't the last person to leave the store. That way she isn't responsible for putting cash in the safe, turning off equipment, and locking doors. She lives alone, so she doesn't worry that her checking rituals will bother anyone. Everything seems good enough as it is.

With time, Tanya starts having more doubts before she leaves the house. Her anxiety intensifies, and her checking routine increases. It becomes a bigger ordeal to leave the house in the morning. The more Tanya checks to relieve her doubt, uncertainty, and anxiety, the more likely she is to check anytime she feels anxious about something bad happening because of her possible negligence. At work, she becomes fearful of pouring coffee from the coffeepot because she worries she might leave too little coffee in the pot, causing it to burn and start a fire. She takes more time to give customers their change because she repeatedly checks to be certain she gives them the correct amount.

Completing stock inventories becomes a nightmare as she repeatedly checks to be certain that she accurately logs incoming and purchased merchandise. Her boss questions why she's spending so much time on details. She's embarrassed to tell him how long she spends repeatedly checking her actions to obtain certainty before moving on to other tasks. The more Tanya checks, the more she sees no way out of her distress but to check some more.

You may know how Tanya feels. She's getting away with her checking compulsions, but she's also feeling the need to check more often and in more situations. Compulsions increasingly interfere with her life. She worries that her symptoms may cause her to lose her job. She can't imagine ever living with someone because she would have to hide her rituals. She debates her situation repeatedly, thinking, *Maybe it's okay to leave things as they are. Or maybe this is going to keep getting worse and I need to do something about it.* Of course, doing something about it probably sounds more distressing than continuing to do what's familiar. It's understandable that Tanya hesitates to start treatment. At the same time, you can see how Tanya's problem worsens as a result of leaving things as they are.

Why Changing the Status Quo Is Worth It

Although it may seem less stressful to leave things as they are, rather than learning to face your fears and change your behaviors, the OCD cycle will worsen if you continue to strengthen it. Life will become more stressful. More aspects of your life will be affected by OCD. Treatment may feel challenging, but it will allow you to break the OCD cycle. The payoff is worth it.

"If I Know My Fears Are OCD, Why Bother Doing ERP?"

It's one thing to understand OCD, and another thing entirely to put that understanding into practice. Unfortunately, understanding OCD on an intellectual level alone won't produce the changes necessary to break the cycle. I wish I could tell you that insight into your symptoms will cause them to go away and that recognizing your symptoms as OCD will help you see that everything is actually okay. It doesn't work that way. The behavioral part of CBT—facing your fears without engaging in compulsions—is the way to make lasting change. Just talking about facing your fears can't do that.

You might use your knowledge about OCD to assuage your OCD-related fears and anxiety. You might tell yourself that there's nothing to worry about because your thoughts and anxiety are "just OCD." This becomes a form of reassurance. But will you ever feel convinced enough that an obsession is "just" an OCD symptom and that you don't need to perform a ritual, seek reassurance, or avoid triggering that thought again? Having knowledge about OCD and understanding your symptoms is a great start, but the work can't stop there. You still need to put that knowledge into practice.

Imagine that you want to learn to dance or play a sport. You read books and gain a good understanding of dance steps or sports moves. But this isn't enough to allow you to perform or play. You need to put what you read into practice—and keep practicing—in order to achieve your goals. Of course, learning to dance or play a sport is a goal you might desire. But learning to face OCD triggers without engaging in compulsions may not sound as appealing! The concept is the same, though: you need to put knowledge into practice to achieve results.

Perhaps physical therapy is a better analogy. Imagine that you hurt your back and your physical therapist explains the importance of doing some painful exercises to strengthen your muscles in order to recover. Doing the exercises may not feel very appealing, but if your back pain is severe enough or interferes with your life, it's probably worth enduring the exercises even though they may be painful in the short term. The long-term gain is worth the short-term pain. Just knowing about your OCD symptoms won't be enough to relieve you of your pain. You have to do the exercises.

Eric: Why Understanding OCD Isn't Enough

Eric suffers from the contamination subtype of OCD. One of his greatest fears is contracting a sexually transmitted disease, especially HIV/AIDS. He avoids walking on certain streets where he has seen syringes on the ground. He avoids walking by certain restaurants and shops because he thinks some of the customers and staff might be at risk for HIV/AIDS. He knows on some level that his fears aren't logical. Seeing a syringe or being in the vicinity of people who he thinks might be at risk for a disease won't somehow contaminate him. He recognizes that his "OCD brain" makes him afraid of these possibilities. As Mary would say, his brain tells him to call 911 when there's no real danger.

In spite of Eric understanding that his thoughts are irrational, what-if questions keep popping into his head and scaring him: *What if someone does have a disease and I get too close? What if my shoe comes too close to a syringe and becomes contaminated? What if my shoe contaminates me? What if I touch something that my shoe touched and I have a tiny cut on my finger that I can't even see? Maybe a virus will get into my bloodstream. How do I know for sure that it won't?* Eric also thinks, *Other people seem to walk by these things and not get anxious. I bet they're not thinking what I'm thinking. I get it: this is my OCD. I'm overestimating the threat and having a hard time tolerating uncertainty. My OCD makes me doubt everything. Still, the threat feels real to me.*

Let's imagine I say to Eric, "That's great that you get it, Eric! The next step is to practice walking on the street that you avoid while facing your fears of contracting a disease because you make that choice. Let's think about walking by those restaurants and shops." Eric says, "No way! It feels too scary to take the risk. I understand that it's my OCD. I get it. I'm going to try not thinking about it so much and not letting it ruin my day. I'm going to remind myself that it's just OCD." This may sound good, but how successful do you think Eric will be when he tries not to think about his fears? Will he be more or less likely to walk in other areas where he sees something that triggers his fears? Without walking on the streets he wants to avoid, Eric won't learn anything new. He won't learn that he can walk on those streets, face his obsessions and anxiety, and not suffer the horrific consequences he fears. Using response prevention, he could learn to accept his fears and refrain from endless avoidance to be certain he doesn't become contaminated.

So now let's imagine that Eric gets on board with treatment. He tells me, "Even though I know this is my OCD, it still feels scary. I know I need to face these doubts and fears to get better. Let's start by walking on the syringe street and then the street with those shops I avoid. Walking by Joe's shop will be the hardest for me, but I'm going to do it. I'm going to face my doubts and uncertainty about being exposed to a deadly disease." In this scenario, Eric isn't avoiding; he's willing to confront triggers of his obsessions, and he's willing to feel the discomfort that comes with facing uncertainty and doubt. He uses his knowledge about OCD to plan ERP practices. He knows he needs to walk the walk (literally!), and he plans to do it.

Why Putting Knowledge into Action Is Worth It

Like many life skills or therapies to heal physical problems, if you don't put what you learn into practice, you don't benefit from what you learn. Understanding OCD is a good start, but to break the OCD cycle, you need to take actions that help you accept frightening obsessions and tolerate the distress they provoke.

"What If Exposure Practices Make My OCD Worse?"

You might think, *But I avoid things because the more I'm triggered, the worse my OCD gets!* You may be concerned that you won't be able to handle the anxiety and discomfort brought on by intentionally facing your fears and think that ERP will make your symptoms worse. You probably have reservations about exposing yourself to challenging situations and intentionally triggering your obsessions. Bear in mind that exposure without response prevention is actually just OCD. Exposure to triggers and obsessions is only half of ERP—the half that creates opportunities to practice response prevention. If you don't refrain from using compulsions, you'll continue to strengthen the OCD cycle. New clients often say, "But I'm not avoiding; I'm exposed to triggers every day and my OCD gets worse." Then, when I ask what they do when faced with triggers of obsessions, I learn about their compulsions and sometimes subtle avoidance strategies. If you encounter triggers every day but don't practice response prevention, your symptoms will worsen.

Most likely, you have a history in which encountering new triggers sets off a spiral of anxiety and compulsions. You probably dread doing that again! You may live in fear of accidentally initiating more OCD episodes. If you've learned that the more you trigger obsessions, the worse you feel and the worse your OCD symptoms become, then of course you wouldn't be inclined to purposely trigger obsessions. So far, exposure to triggers probably only made things worse for you. Mary's story is a great example of how the OCD cycle worsens if exposure to triggers isn't accompanied by response prevention. When new situations triggered her anxiety, Mary frantically washed and tried to avoid more triggers. The more she washed and engaged in avoidance, the worse her symptoms became. Before long, almost every situation and person in her life was a potential trigger for another OCD episode that led to frantic efforts to wash away feelings of contamination. Of course, Mary didn't yet know about or understand the concept of response prevention. She was frightened and did what felt intuitive: she tried to wash and clean to feel better and avoid triggering more episodes.

Practicing new responses is the goal of ERP. Your initial practices will be carefully planned, and you'll play a key role in planning them. Eventually, you'll be able to apply what you learn to spontaneous triggers that surprise you, coming from out of the blue during the course of a day. As Mary would say, you'll stop reacting to every garden hose as if it were a snake. Starting to practice new responses to obsessions and urges to engage in compulsions takes courage. It feels scary to risk triggering an onslaught of anxiety and urges to use compulsions, but your goal is response prevention, allowing you to practice new responses when your obsessions are triggered.

EXERCISE: Identifying How You Want to Live Your Life

If ERP sounds frightening because you're afraid to take the risk of intentionally triggering obsessions, try thinking about the bigger picture and how you want to live your life. You may think you're playing it safe by trying to avoid obsessions, but in fact, not only does this strengthen the hold your symptoms have on you, it also limits your possibilities in life. In this exercise (inspired by Mooney and Padesky 2000), you'll picture someone who lives more the way you want to live and imagine how that person would face the challenge of accepting uncertainty and doubt. Try to identify a specific role model or character, an ideal fictional or non-fictional figure who seems to live life the way you want to live, such as a political or sports figure, a character in a movie, or a personal mentor. Imagining a role model's actions can help you courageously move toward choices that you want to make but feel nervous about.

Take some time now to write in your journal about this person and the possibilities for how you'd like to live your life. If you acted more like the person you admire, what might your life look like? Although you're using a role model for this exercise, remember that the goal here is to write about how **you** would like to live your life.

Now imagine that person having OCD and facing the decision to commit to ERP. How would that person handle fears about ERP? Would that person willingly face uncertainty and doubt in order to open up new possibilities in life? Would that person choose to take on ERP in spite of fears about triggering obsessions? Does taking a cue from the attitudes and behaviors of someone you admire help you find courage to commit to difficult tasks?

Here are some examples of what other people with OCD wrote when doing this exercise:

> I've read a lot about Eleanor Roosevelt, and I'd like to be more like her. If she was afraid of a challenge, I bet she did things anyway. Just because thoughts scare me, I don't want them to control me. I want to feel strong and confident. I want to face what scares me and carry on with my life. I picture Mrs. Roosevelt telling obsessive thoughts, "Come on, give me what you got! I can handle you!" I want to be like that.

I imagine this one action hero in my favorite movie. When the going gets tough, he never backs away. He makes some funny crack about what he's up against and then goes for it. Of course, movies aren't real life, but I need to be more like an action hero to face OCD. People without OCD don't understand how much courage it takes to do ERP. I feel like it sometimes takes all the courage I have to not give in to compulsions. I want to be courageous and face challenges rather than back away from them. I want to be more like that guy.

Why Facing Your Fears Is Worth It

Exposure without response prevention will strengthen OCD. When you practice ERP, you learn to face obsessions and discomfort without engaging in compulsions. As you begin facing uncertainty and doubt rather than escaping from it, you open up possibilities that allow you to embark on a path of living life the way you want to live.

"What If I'm Not Careful Enough and Something Bad Does Happen?"

It feels scary to give up compulsions. Almost all of my clients express concern that if they do so, something bad could happen. One reason you may engage in compulsions is because you believe that if you don't, something bad might happen and you'll be responsible. Or you may fear that the discomfort of not engaging in compulsions could be too terrible to bear and you'll be completely unable to function. Giving up compulsions can feel like intentionally taking big risks. You may question if the stakes are too high. You may dread the thought of taking actions that cause you to feel irresponsible or capable of doing dangerous things. Do any of the following concerns sound familiar?

◆ *If I'm less careful about what I touch and how often I wash my hands, how far will I go? Will I become careless and start risking my health and my family's health?*

- *If I stop checking appliances and locks before I leave the house, what if I eventually become irresponsible?*

- *If I become less anxious about the thought of killing my husband, isn't that a bad thing? I should feel anxious, right? If these thoughts don't bother me so much, wouldn't that mean I really could be capable of murder?*

- *If I get comfortable with things being out of order, I might become disorganized. My home and office could become a mess.*

The underlying theme of these concerns is *How far in the other direction will I go if I resist compulsions?* Clients often say they fear becoming the opposite of who they are now—becoming irresponsible, immoral, disorganized, or an excessive risk taker. This is *all-or-nothing thinking*, meaning they think they'll be at either one end of the continuum or the other. It doesn't work that way. Treatment doesn't make you become the opposite of who you are and behave in ways contradictory to what you value. ERP doesn't take away your personality; rather, it helps you be the person you want to be: someone who is better able to take appropriate risks without excessive anxiety. If responsibility is an important value to you, you'll continue to be a responsible person. If organization is important to you, you'll continue to be an organized person. The goal of treatment is to be less gripped by fear and more able to respond to thoughts in a flexible and balanced way.

Let's think about contamination fears. Although it's true that you may be exposed to germs, it's also true that everyone is exposed to germs a great deal of the time. Treatment will help you take risks that people without OCD take every day. ERP doesn't mean intentionally injecting yourself with a dreaded virus to learn you can handle it; it means taking the risks that everyone takes in life and tolerating a degree of uncertainty to do so. We are all exposed to germs and viruses. Sometimes people get sick. Consider the benefits of taking the same risks that everybody takes without overfocusing on what-ifs, seeking certainty, and using compulsions and avoidance maneuvers at every turn.

One of the hardest fears to handle is the one people with aggressive, sexual, or blasphemous thoughts face: *If I decrease my anxiety and accept thoughts about killing my spouse, molesting children, or offending God, isn't that a bad thing? Aren't those thoughts that we shouldn't have? If I become less anxious about these thoughts or images, won't that mean I'm a socio-path, capable of harming people, or a sinner? Why would I want to be less anxious about horrible thoughts of doing unspeakable acts against vulnerable people, children, or even God?* If being a responsible person who doesn't intentionally harm others or commit grievous sins is an important value to you, then it still will be after ERP. Although certain thoughts may always bother you, the meaning you attach to them will lessen. You'll learn that you can live with disturbing thoughts without them meaning something horrible about you. Some thoughts may always feel unpleasant and anxiety provoking to some degree, but they can be nothing more than unpleasant thoughts with no special meaning. Remember, people who don't have OCD have disturbing and horrible thoughts too. The difference is that they don't attach much meaning and importance to those thoughts. How you interpret and respond to intrusive thoughts is what matters.

Why Accepting Scary Thoughts Is Worth It

ERP teaches you that you can accept thoughts that scare you without responding to them as emergencies. Although bad things do happen in life, you can live your life without the burden of always trying to control or prevent the catastrophes you fear. You don't need to make thoughts go away. You also don't need to interpret them as dangerous, like you do now. You won't become the opposite of the person you are and behave in ways contrary to what you value. You'll stay true to your values, but you won't fear intrusive thoughts just because they're at odds with what you deem to be important.

"If I Face My Fears, Won't New Ones Pop Up?"

Like the game whack-a-mole, in OCD you can whack one mole, decreasing anxiety about one obsession, only to have another one pop up.

People sometimes think that CBT won't work because it focuses on symptoms, and if you don't treat the root of the problem, new OCD symptoms will just spring up somewhere else. While it's true that symptoms take many forms and are likely to change or morph at different points in time, their underlying themes remain the same. How you respond to underlying themes is at the root of the problem in OCD. Themes of uncertainty, perfectionism, overestimation of responsibility and threat, and interpreting thoughts as overly important can each take many forms. Triggers of these underlying themes can pop up anywhere and at any time. Your brain grabs onto thoughts that feel important and frightening. Those thoughts can stick. Your mind may find a new angle to an intrusive thought that frightens you even more.

CBT targets the themes underlying your symptoms. The content of your obsessions and compulsions provides opportunities to practice changing your responses to those underlying themes. In the process, you become armed with an approach that will work for facing any obsession that might surface. The goal isn't to stop thoughts or images from running through your mind, like new moles popping up; the goal is to build confidence in facing those thoughts and images whenever they pop up and whatever form they take.

Imagine no longer living in fear of triggering obsessions because you know how to handle them. Imagine not feeling the need to be hypervigilant about triggering another dreaded OCD fear. Although you may not always know what form an obsession will take or what compulsion you may be tempted to perform, you can build confidence in your ability to handle thoughts and images and the related anxiety or discomfort without performing compulsions. Knowing that you can handle underlying OCD themes differently than you do now will help you feel prepared to handle any intrusive thought that frightens you.

Knowing that other obsessions might pop up in the future, you might feel discouraged by the prospect of going through ERP and having to face future triggers without using compulsions. But consider the bigger picture. Ask yourself, *What matters to me more than engaging in compulsions and avoidance? What do I value more than avoiding the anxiety and discomfort associated with my obsessions?* Many of my clients find these questions to be helpful in building the courage to face obsessions head-on, whenever and wherever they're triggered. Clarifying your values can help you choose to take actions, including doing ERP now and in the future, that help you live the life you want. In his memoir *Rewind, Replay, Repeat*, Jeff Bell (2007) describes how stuck he felt until he realized the value of the greater good (enhancing his sense of purpose and service to others) in motivating himself to successfully face his doubts and take actions in line with his values. By clarifying your values *now*, you can increase your motivation to face your fears right from the start of treatment.

EXERCISE: Clarifying What a Valued Life Looks Like for You

Acceptance and commitment therapy (ACT) emphasizes the benefit of living a life that's true to your values. This approach requires willingness to take valued actions and making a commitment to do so (Hayes, Strosahl, and Wilson 1999). An exercise from ACT that many people find helpful is to imagine what they'd like written on their tombstone when they die, or what they hope loved ones will say about them in a eulogy. In his book **Get Out of Your Mind and Into Your Life**, Steven Hayes, one of the creators of ACT, asks, "What would you like your life to stand for?" (2005, 170).

Take some time to consider your response to this powerful question, then record your thoughts in your journal. What do you want your life to stand for? Do you want to be remembered for being anxious, engaging in compulsions, and avoiding people because of your OCD? Would you prefer to be remembered for qualities such as being a supportive friend, a loving parent, or a person who lived life fully? Does OCD interfere with living in alignment with your values? As you write on this topic, think about your values in various life domains, such as intimate relationships, parenting, friendships, career or education, personal growth, recreation and leisure time, health, spirituality, or any other domains of life that are important to you. Try writing your own epitaph or eulogy, and write two versions: one that reflects your life as you're living now, trapped in the OCD cycle, and one in which you're living in alignment with your values. (You can find information about ACT and building willingness to take committed action toward living a life that you value in the ACT books listed in the Resources section at the end of this book.)

Here's an example written by Wayne, an unmarried computer programmer who used to enjoy spending time with his friends, using the approach of writing his own eulogy.

Eulogy for Wayne, Who Suffered from OCD

Poor Wayne, he always seemed anxious and spent lots of time doing things in his own special way. He avoided going out with his friends because so many places made him feel unclean or contaminated. He used to want a family, but he never married because he didn't want anyone interfering with his compulsions. He didn't let many people into his world. He used to be a warm and loving friend, but the more he suffered from OCD, the more distant he became.

Eulogy for Wayne, Who Broke Free from the Cycle of OCD

Wayne enjoyed life and faced challenges with courage and determination. He prioritized his friends and enjoyed activities that brought people together. He cherished his wife, Eileen, and his beautiful son, Luke. Wayne was a warm and loving husband, father, and friend. People enjoyed his company. We all can learn from how he lived his life. He was a true inspiration.

I'm guessing that living your life at the mercy of obsessions, compulsions, and desires to avoid people and places that matter to you isn't in line with what you truly value. When you clarify your values, you're likely to see a discrepancy between what life looks like when you allow obsessions, compulsions, and avoidance to yank you around and what life could look like if you commit to taking actions to overcome OCD, including any new fears that arise in the future.

Why Willingness to Face New Fears Is Worth It

While it's true that new obsessions or triggers of obsessions may pop up at any time, it's also true that by learning to face the themes underlying your OCD, you'll develop confidence in your ability to handle them differently whenever and however they arise. ERP uses your current obsessions and situations to help you develop those skills, but the skills are yours for life. If you maintain your gains by using response prevention whenever either old or new obsessions trigger anxiety or discomfort, you'll remain free to live a life that you value.

"Can't I Get Better Some Other Way?"

It's tempting to look for ways around doing ERP and facing your fears. As discussed in chapter 3, medication can be effective for some people, especially when anxiety feels so intolerable that they can't effectively engage in treatment, or when they have other problems, such as depression, that make it hard to function or do ERP. In those situations, medication can provide some essential relief. But if you want to learn to break the OCD cycle and build lifelong skills for doing so, CBT (with or without medication) will give you the tools you need to face intrusive thoughts and respond in new ways, without engaging in compulsions, now and in the future. It may be tempting to try less anxiety-provoking treatment approaches. But if they haven't been shown to be effective, why not start with one that has? Avoiding the treatment shown to be most effective for OCD may be another form of avoidance of facing your fears, which only strengthens the OCD cycle.

EXERCISE: Imagining How Your Life Could Look Different Than It Does Now

To face the short-term discomforts of ERP, it helps to imagine your life, in vivid detail, without OCD running it. I often ask my clients, "If we're successful in our work together, what will be different? How will you know we've been successful?" Imagining a life that isn't controlled by your OCD can be motivating and provide great incentive for taking on the hard work ahead. What better way to decide if ERP is worth doing than to think about how your life could be different after you finish treatment? Despite the challenges you'll face with ERP, will it be worth it to have your life back, to spend time with loved ones without engaging in compulsions, or to not feel you must avoid people or places that you used to enjoy? Imagine your day-to-day life without feeling at the mercy of obsessions or compulsions, then spend some time writing in your journal about what you envision. The following questions may help you envision that future more fully:

- What will your days look like if you don't spend so much time performing compulsions?

- How will you feel throughout the day if you aren't terrified about triggering obsessions?

- What will you do that you don't feel you can do now because of your OCD symptoms? What will you do with the free time you gain—time that's currently consumed by thinking about obsessions and engaging in compulsions?

Here are a couple of examples of what other people with OCD wrote when they did this exercise:

I'll enjoy my life! I won't have to hide my compulsions from everybody at work. I won't ask for reassurance from my wife every day. I won't ask her to leave her shoes outside, wash her hands after touching anything I think is contaminated, or handle food super carefully. We'll entertain and have people over to our house for dinner. I won't take so long in the bathroom doing my rituals. My hands will finally heal after all of this hand washing. Maybe we can plan a trip. That will make my wife so happy! Seeing her happy and not frustrated by my OCD will make me happy.

I won't be so terrified to be around my nieces and nephews. I won't walk around lost in thoughts about whether or not I'm capable of harming people. I won't avoid people. I'll make dinner and chop vegetables with knives even if my husband is nearby. I won't cry at night wondering how I can know for sure that I won't do something horrible. I'll go to movies again and be able to watch television shows without holding my breath to see if something will trigger my anxiety and ruin the rest of my evening.

Why Doing ERP Is Worth It

You can try using other approaches to treat OCD, but if you're trying to avoid facing your fears, then you're likely to continue strengthening the OCD cycle. CBT approaches help you break the cycle and open up possibilities for how you live your life.

Summary

You probably have questions that make you hesitate about starting treatment. You may want certainty that treatment will be worth it. This wouldn't be surprising, given that intolerance of uncertainty is a core problem for people with OCD. I encourage you to remember all of the reasons why treatment is worth doing, despite the difficulty and uncertainty. Review your responses to the exercises in this chapter and chapter 3, and discuss them with a therapist who's trained in treating OCD or with supportive family members and friends who can help you think through why the challenges of treatment are worth it to you. Focus on what's more important to you than continuing to respond to intrusive thoughts with compulsions or avoidance. What would a valued life look like for you if you break free from the OCD cycle? All of this will help you commit to treatment. It takes courage to face your fears head-on. I hope you decide it's worth it.

In chapter 5, I'll explain what your initial treatment sessions might be like and how you might start ERP. It may not be as frightening as you fear. Hopefully that too will help you commit to seeking treatment and building the life you dream of for yourself.

CHAPTER 5

GETTING STARTED WITH EXPOSURE AND RESPONSE PREVENTION

Hopefully you're ready to start treatment. Yet you may still wonder what ERP will look like for you. I imagine my clients think something like this: *Okay, my therapist seems nice. She understands my symptoms. I get the rationale for this treatment. Self-help books describe how this is going to go. I'll make a list of my obsessions and what I'm afraid will happen if I don't use compulsions. I'll face my fears and not engage in compulsions or avoidance. I'll learn that I can handle anxiety and that my fears aren't likely to be realized. I get the concept, but what is it really like? What kinds of things will I have to do?*

In this chapter, I discuss the nitty-gritty details of ERP. Of course, each person's OCD triggers, obsessions, and compulsions are different, so no two courses of treatment will be identical. For example, imagine two people who wash their hands throughout the day to avoid contamination by germs. One person rates touching the doorknob of the public restroom at my office suite as a 20 on the subjective units of discomfort (SUDS) scale and fears feeling uncomfortable until she washes her hands, while another person rates touching the same doorknob as a 60 on the SUDS scale and fears contaminating objects that will enter his home. The first person avoids touching the handle completely or only touches it using her sleeve, while the second person might touch the handle but then not touch items he brings into his home until he washes his hands in a ritualized fashion.

In addition, therapists specializing in ERP bring different styles to treatment. All will help you target the same underlying themes, but the nuances in how they do that can vary. For example, Mary's therapist uses metaphors to explain the OCD cycle and how treatment works and teaches creative strategies to lean in toward fears, whereas another therapist might offer a more nuts-and-bolts approach. Most therapists will practice ERP with you in the office. Some will ask you to practice on your own earlier in treatment than others. Some will join you outside of the office to practice. Different therapists will offer different suggestions about how to target your core fears. Your therapist may suggest watching videos that trigger obsessions, saying or writing feared or avoided words, going to certain locations to practice, or writing scripts for imaginal exposure to feared scenarios. Yet in all cases, the goal is the same: facing obsessions and tolerating discomfort without engaging in compulsions so you can change your expectations about the consequences of facing your fears. There can be many avenues to achieving that goal.

Initial Sessions

In addition to signing informed consent forms, completing questionnaires, and providing your symptom history, in the first session or two you and your therapist will get to know each other and discuss treatment. Your therapist will answer your questions and describe what treatment will be like. If you're hesitant to begin, you can discuss your concerns and try to resolve some of your ambivalence. If you decide to move forward, you might begin by monitoring your symptoms.

Monitoring

Monitoring your obsessions and compulsions will help you design and personalize your treatment plan. You might be tempted to skip this step because you think you have a good understanding of the many triggers, thoughts, and compulsions you struggle with. It can be an eye-opening exercise to monitor and record your symptoms. You may discover compulsions or avoidance behaviors that are so automatic that you hadn't been noticing them.

Here's how Mary described what happened when she started monitoring her symptoms:

The simple act of avoiding was such an ingrained habit. My therapist said I should start writing down what I avoided and how I did it. This sounded like an easy task, but it turned out to be not so easy because I'd rather avoid things than notice what I'm avoiding! He also asked me to write down rituals I performed, such as showering or washing my clothes. The first day I attempted to do this, I was astounded by how many times I engaged in compulsions and avoidance and exhausted from paying attention to it. I could have written all day!

I decided to write down major things and just notice minor ones. Driving to work the next morning, I noticed that I did an "inward cringe" when I drove under a highway bridge. There are quite a few homeless people living under the bridge, so I cringed to avoid seeing them. When I arrived at work I noticed that I didn't want to touch the back door handle because that's where the smokers hang out. It seemed dirty to me, so I usually pushed the door open without touching the handle and washed my hands before sitting down at my computer. I avoided walking by a certain person's office because I deemed him unclean. I moved a Japanese screen divider to block a messy, unorganized area of the office from my view at my desk, and I wiped my desk with Clorox wipes. It wasn't even ten in the morning! I had my homework cut out for me.

Gina's therapist gave her a monitoring form and asked her to assign SUDS ratings to her levels of distress using a scale of 100, where 0 is no distress and 100 is the greatest distress possible. Like Mary, Gina found it difficult to write down triggering situations and her disturbing thoughts. She was accustomed to trying to *not* think about thoughts that tormented her. It makes sense that monitoring anxiety-provoking situations and thoughts would be anxiety provoking. After all, it requires you to pay attention to sources of anxiety instead of trying to avoid them. This means turning toward your fears instead of away from them, which can be a hard step to take at first. But this will be an important step in your recovery. You might not feel quite ready to do this now, but taking a close look at your obsessions and the range of your compulsions and avoidance behaviors will allow you to individualize your treatment plan and change your responses to your obsessions.

EXERCISE: Monitoring Your OCD Triggers, Obsessions, Compulsions, and Avoidance

If you feel ready to monitor your obsessions, compulsions, avoidance behaviors, and the situations that trigger them, use your journal to jot down your observations of these events over the course of a day. Like Ted, you may have already begun to monitor your symptoms. Or maybe you feel like Gina and want to avoid paying attention to triggers of intrusive thoughts. You may relate to Mary's experience if you engage in so many compulsions and so much avoidance that it seems nearly impossible to record everything.

Monitoring even just some of your obsessions, compulsions, and avoidance behaviors can increase your awareness of them and the situations that trigger them. You might start to see that some triggers and obsessions are more anxiety provoking than others. You might develop a better understanding of what you fear and expect will happen if you don't engage in compulsions. In your journal, also write about what you learn from your monitoring, including any patterns you notice. Take these notes to your therapy appointment.

If you find it difficult to do this monitoring right now, that's okay. Your therapist can help you figure out how to best monitor your symptoms and overcome obstacles to monitoring.

Creating Your Game Plan

Although Ted started treatment with an ERP hierarchy in hand, you'll probably create your hierarchy with the help of your therapist. Once you list situations and thoughts to face and compulsions to eliminate, you can work together to decide where to start. In the examples that follow, hierarchies of four people with different subtypes of OCD illustrate what initial hierarchy items might look like. Later in the chapter, I'll return to the four people in these examples, discussing how their OCD manifests and outlining ERP planning and early treatment for each.

Because new research developments show that the effectiveness of exposure-based treatment appears to be due to the fact that it violates expectations people have about facing fears, your therapist may also ask you to track shifts in your expectations about negative outcomes during ERP (Abramowitz and Arch 2014). For example, you may start an ERP session believing that you won't be able to tolerate discomfort when touching something dirty for more than a few seconds, but then once you learn you can, your expectations about how long you can touch such objects and tolerate your feelings change. Consistent with recent research on exposure-based treatment, your therapist may guide you through practicing ERP at various levels on your hierarchy rather than working systematically from easier to harder items. The goal is to facilitate new learning about your fears and retrieve what you learn no matter what level of distress you encounter and no matter where and when you encounter triggers of obsessions.

Kim: Contamination Obsessions

Situations (to be faced without washing or using other compulsions)	SUDS
Touch forms in my therapist's office.	15
Touch the desk in my therapist's office.	20
Touch door handles in my therapist's office suite.	30
Use the door keypad at my therapist's office.	40
Sit on benches on the sidewalk.	45
Touch money and pay using cash.	55
Open the door to women's restrooms in nice restaurants.	65
Open the door to women's restrooms in public parks.	80
Flush toilets and leave the women's restroom without using paper towels to touch anything.	90
Use the restroom at a doctor's office where other patients might be ill.	100

Sammy: Responsibility for Harm or Mistakes Obsessions

Situations	SUDS
Don't check or stare to see if the refrigerator door is closed.	10
Don't check to be certain the bathroom faucets are turned off.	15
Don't check to be sure small appliances are unplugged.	20
Don't check or stare to be certain the coffeemaker is unplugged.	30
Don't check windows or use rituals when closing them.	40

Don't check to be certain that the stove is turned off.	45
Don't check door locks or use rituals when bolting them.	55
Don't double-check to be sure file cabinets at work are locked.	65
Mail envelopes without checking to be certain of their contents.	70
Don't circle back when I feel a bump in the road on a quiet street.	85
Don't circle back when I feel a bump in the road on a busy street with pedestrians.	100

Jennifer: Aggressive Thoughts

Situations (to be faced without seeking reassurance or using other compulsions)	SUDS
Repeat the word "knife."	30
Repeat the words "stab," "murderer," and "killer."	35
Listen to a song with aggressive lyrics.	40
Watch a TV show about a woman who murders.	55
Look up stories on the Internet about real women murderers.	65
Hold a knife and say "murderer."	75
Write and imagine the scenario of stabbing my husband.	80
Repeat imagining the stabbing scenario while using knives at home around my husband.	90
Write and imagine the scenario of being misdiagnosed and really being a killer.	95
Write and imagine the scenario of never knowing if I could be a murderer.	100

Cooper: Symmetry and "Just Right" Obsessions

Situations (to be faced without correcting, redoing, or using other compulsions)	SUDS
Write sentences imperfectly and not centered on the page.	25–30
End the last line of a paragraph near the top of a page.	35
Make mistakes when writing checks.	40
Send imperfect e-mails to my therapist.	45
Start but don't finish reading magazine articles.	50
Send imperfect e-mails to friends.	55
End work reports on an odd-numbered page.	65
Don't check work e-mails to be sure they're written perfectly.	75–80
Limit work reports to one read through.	90
Don't ask for reassurance at work about how I've written something.	100

It can be difficult to create a hierarchy when new and different spontaneous triggers occur almost nonstop throughout the day. Mary was plagued by feelings of contamination and uncertainty that were triggered by almost anything she encountered. Instead of choosing to face specific items on a hierarchy, she and her therapist decided it made more sense to start with practices of leaning in toward current disturbing images that frightened her due to uncertainty about what she had seen. Then they chose homework practices that involved decreasing avoidance and reducing washing rituals throughout the day whenever she encountered triggers of her fears.

Gina and her therapist decided to begin with a hierarchy of items that triggered her doubts about being gay, mainly because at that time those doubts were more intense and disruptive to her life than her harming fears. If you struggle with more than one type of obsession, it can be best to tackle them one at a time. There are different ways to approach this choice: You might start with less anxiety-provoking obsessions, or you might choose to target obsessions that currently cause the most suffering and disruption in your life. Ted and his therapist agreed to begin with lower hierarchy items, which involved imaginal exposures to past situations and both imaginal and real-life practices with current obsessions. In chapter 6, you'll see how Mary, Gina, and Ted put ERP into action. For now, we'll look at how you and your therapist might plan initial practices.

EXERCISE: Brainstorming Ideas for Your Game Plan

You may have ideas about items to include on your exposure hierarchy. You might have thoughts about a game plan for changing your responses to obsessions and urges to use compulsions. If so, write them in your journal. Thinking about and recording these ideas will facilitate discussing them with your therapist. It will also help you begin to play an active role in your treatment. ERP feels much more manageable when you realize how much of a role you play in designing your hierarchy and choosing your practices. The following questions may help you come up with some ideas:

◆ Does Mary's plan to begin ERP by reducing compulsions rather than eliminating them altogether seem like a good place for you to start?

◆ Do your obsessions involve more than one category, like Gina's did? If so, do you have thoughts about which one you'd like to start tackling and why?

◆ Do your obsessions involve doubts about past and current situations like Ted's did? If so, does it seem more manageable to start by facing certain doubts before tackling others?

◆ Do some compulsions seem easier to start eliminating than others? Do any compulsions interfere with your life so much that you'd like to start by reducing those, even if the thought of doing so is more distressing?

Planning ERP

Making an effective ERP plan is key to treatment success. In this section, I'll discuss several key factors to consider in your planning:

- Choosing triggers and obsessions for ERP practices

- Choosing response prevention goals and identifying expectations about the feared consequences

- Leaning in toward obsessions and not using safety behaviors

- Deciding on therapist-assisted practices, homework, and practicing on your own

Choosing Triggers and Obsessions for ERP

Before you begin an ERP session, you'll choose triggers and obsessions to intentionally face. You'll work with your therapist to choose items on your hierarchy that make good sense for you to start with. The goal is to increase your anxiety or discomfort enough to learn what happens when you ride it out and face your fear instead of engaging in a compulsion. For the same reason, you don't want to take on a practice that feels too distressing if you're likely to give in to compulsions; that will only strengthen the OCD cycle. Where you start will be up to you and your therapist. You may prefer to start with relatively easy items, or you may feel willing to begin with items that are in the middle of your hierarchy and stagger your practices right from the start. You may choose items that are a bit harder than others but have a more detrimental effect on your life.

Choosing Response Prevention Goals and Identifying Expectations About Feared Consequences

ERP practices should be designed to challenge your core fears and expectations. Sometimes fears are specific, such as *If I don't tap in counts of four, something horrible will happen to my family.* Sometimes they're vague, such as *If I don't tap in fours, something bad will happen. I don't know what it will be, but it will be my fault.* And sometimes the feared consequences are even less clear. You might anticipate feelings of anxiety and think, *If I don't tap in fours, it will feel wrong and uncomfortable. I don't know how bad the feeling will get or how long I'll be able to handle it.*

The more clear you are about what you fear, the better you'll understand the beliefs you're challenging and the new response you want to practice. If you fear that something bad will happen to your family, response prevention will involve not tapping in counts of four and instead sitting with feelings of uncertainty that something could happen to your family. If you fear not being able to tolerate anxiety or discomfort associated with uncertainty for more than a few seconds, response prevention will involve not tapping in fours and instead sitting with uncomfortable feelings and uncertainty about how bad your feelings might get for a designated time that's longer than a few seconds.

If it feels too hard to completely refrain from a compulsion, you can set a goal that modifies how you perform that compulsion. For example, if you engage in lengthy hand washing rituals lasting about four minutes, you may find it too difficult to completely refrain from washing your hands after exposure to feelings of contamination. If washing for two and a half minutes instead of four seems hard to tolerate or raises a significant amount of anxiety but feels like something you're willing to face, that may be a good goal for that session. As long as you complete ERP practices having changed your responses to obsessions and having learned something new about what happens if you do, you've done well.

As for duration of ERP sessions, ideally you want to end a practice after new learning occurs and you see that the consequences of facing fears instead of using compulsions or avoidance are not what you expected. This extends to beliefs about your ability to tolerate uncomfortable and frightening feelings. You want to learn that you can tolerate difficult feelings and challenge beliefs associated with uncertainty, imperfection, responsibility and threat, or the importance of your thoughts. It might be tempting to bail out when you feel really uncomfortable, but it's important to resist that urge. That's exactly what you've been doing, and it only deepens the OCD cycle. When you trigger an obsession and feel extremely uncomfortable, your therapist will encourage you to hang in there and ride out the discomfort long enough to challenge your beliefs. If you try to escape the anxiety too soon, you'll strengthen your belief that you can't handle it and that your feared consequences of not using compulsions or avoidance may be true.

Leaning In Toward Obsessions and Not Using Safety Behaviors

It's one thing to say you're going to face a trigger and bring on an obsession, but it's another thing altogether to tolerate anxiety and uncertainty about feared consequences. However, if you're only halfway committed when doing ERP, you won't benefit from treatment. For ERP to work, you need to face your fears and not look for shortcuts. It may be tempting to "cheat." It's not uncommon for people to use avoidance maneuvers, such as distraction or reassurance seeking, to avoid feeling anxious or uncomfortable. It's natural to try to think about something else or mentally try to reassure yourself that everything is okay, especially because you've used these strategies for a long time. But these safety behaviors haven't worked, and they'll prevent you from fully accepting your thoughts and feelings and challenging your expectations about what will happen during ERP. When you're ready to put ERP into practice, it may help to review your responses to the exercises in chapters 3 and 4 as a reminder of why it's worth it to fully lean in toward what makes you uncomfortable.

Deciding on Therapist-Assisted Practices, Homework, and Practicing on Your Own

It can be frightening and confusing to start ERP. If it was easy to resist compulsions, you would already have done so! Your therapist can guide you as you choose ERP practices and will probably be with you as you begin the process of learning to face obsessions without engaging in compulsions or any safety behaviors. Eventually, though, your therapist's presence will only serve to help you feel safe and therefore will interfere with fully engaging in ERP—you might think, *If my therapist is watching me do these things, it must be safe. She would never let me take a real risk. I can trust her judgment even if I can't trust my own.* Your therapist's role will therefore shift during treatment, and sooner or later you'll practice ERP on your own.

Practicing ERP between sessions will be just as important as what you do in session, if not more important. Your therapist will help you plan homework practices that build on in-session exposures. You'll make plans to maximize the likelihood that you'll successfully complete ERP practices for homework. Your challenge will be to practice frequently and consistently outside of therapy sessions. As you learn to lean in toward obsessions and not use safety behaviors, you'll take on increasing responsibility for practicing on your own. However, the transition to practicing on your own can feel frightening. Your therapist will encourage and support your efforts and will help you troubleshoot obstacles.

Mary had been nervous about starting ERP homework but told me, "Discussing it with my therapist helped me not feel so isolated. I wouldn't be doing this on my own. I'd be reporting back and telling him about it. Even though I'd be alone when I was doing the exposure, he would be with me in spirit. In the beginning, that helped carry me through it. Later, leaning in toward obsessions on my own just became a natural thing I did."

Starting ERP

Before my clients begin an ERP session, they often ask, "Why did I say that I'm willing to do this?" It's normal to feel anxious before starting ERP. I encourage you to repeatedly review the reasons why you decided that treatment is worth it to you. And remember, whether to take on an ERP practice is always your decision. Also, you don't have to take on everything on your hierarchy at once. You might choose to face multiple situations later in treatment, but you can take it one step at a time in the beginning.

In the four examples that follow, which involve the same four people whose hierarchies appeared earlier in the chapter, you'll see how ERP typically starts by taking one step at a time. The people in these stories are beginning to do ERP for contamination fears, responsibility beliefs, aggressive thoughts, and symmetry or "just right" obsessions. Your ERP approach won't look exactly like any of these examples, but they will probably give you some ideas about how to creatively plan your own ERP practices. In addition, your therapist will guide you in designing ERP practices personalized to fit your obsessions. While it's fine to jump ahead to examples that correspond to the content of your obsessions, I encourage you to read all four examples, as the overall approach is similar for all subtypes of OCD.

Kim: ERP for Contamination Obsessions

Kim suffers from contamination obsessions. She fears coming into contact with germs and avoids touching almost everything in public locations. She washes her hands as soon as possible after touching anything that makes her feel contaminated. For someone like Kim, coming to my office is stressful because it involves exposure to numerous triggers, including touching the keypad and door latch to enter the waiting room and sitting in chairs where others have sat. It takes courage for Kim to start treatment. She uses her sleeve to open doors and uses sanitizing hand wipes as soon as she leaves the office.

PLANNING ERP FOR CONTAMINATION OBSESSIONS

Kim can start ERP with hierarchy items that we can practice in my office. Using the SUDS scale, she rated touching a form in my office as a 15 and touching my desk as a 20. Kim has two core fears about touching these items: that she'll become contaminated, and that she'll feel so anxious about contamination that she won't be able to handle it. Kim needs to confront her uncertainty about possibly becoming contaminated and her expectation that she can't handle the anxiety if she feels contaminated.

We decide to start with therapist-assisted practices in session and then plan homework practices that Kim will complete on her own. We set aside enough time in the session for her to successfully complete an initial ERP practice. We wouldn't want to end the session when she's highly anxious, since stopping ERP could be seen as an opportunity to escape from her high anxiety. However, if Kim had learned that she could handle anxiety, it would be okay to end the session before her anxiety dissipates.

Kim knows that she'll be tempted to reassure herself that everything is okay because she's in my office and I won't let anything bad happen to her. She also knows that she'll be tempted to make a backup plan to use sanitizing hand wipes before she gets to her car and possibly wash her clothes when she gets home. Ideally, we'll identify any safety behaviors and strategize to help her not engage in reassurance seeking or backup planning to use compulsions. Throughout the session, I'll check in to be sure Kim isn't avoiding frightening thoughts and feelings.

STARTING ERP FOR CONTAMINATION OBSESSIONS

Kim rates her anxiety as higher than usual because of starting ERP. When she's ready to begin, we start the first agreed-upon practice. I ask Kim if she's ready to touch one of my office forms. She brings her hand close to the form but doesn't touch it. I ask Kim what she's thinking, and she tells me, "I don't know who else might have touched the form. It feels scary to touch it." I ask her to tell me what she fears, and she replies, "I'll feel contaminated. I'll keep thinking that maybe I just did something that I knew I shouldn't have done. I know it sounds crazy, but what if someone other than you printed these forms? What if I touch something that a stranger touched?"

Instead of reassuring Kim, I want to help her confront her fears. I think about the underlying themes that we're targeting and say, "Kim, we actually want to think about the possibility that these forms might be contaminated and that you might be exposed to germs. We just can't know for certain, right?" Because our discussion had prepared Kim for this practice, she says, "Right. I want to tell myself that there are no germs on the forms, but I know that's looking for reassurance. Okay, these forms might be contaminated. That makes me anxious." I encourage Kim to stay with these thoughts and feelings. Her anxiety starts going down, but then she tells me it's getting higher again because she's thinking about touching the form.

When Kim is ready, she touches the form with one finger and then pulls her finger away. I ask her if she can keep her finger on the form. When she does, she grimaces and tells me, "Okay, this is uncomfortable now." I say, "Great!" Then I check with Kim and ask her why she thinks I said "great" when she told me how uncomfortable she felt. She says, "Because I'm doing it! I'm confronting my fears. I'm thinking about this form being full of germs and how I might be contaminating myself."

I continue to ask Kim about her feelings as she fully leans in to her fears and anxiety. Kim says, "It's really not so bad now," so I ask if she's ready to touch the form with her whole hand. When Kim decides she's ready, she puts her whole hand on the form and leaves it there. I ask her to tell me what she's leaning in toward. She says, "I don't know if I'm contaminated. I'm going to live with the uncertainty. Maybe I'll find out that I contracted a virus, and maybe it will be because of this moment right now. I'll never know." Kim starts to smile and says, "The longer I keep my hand here, the easier it gets." With that, Kim successfully completes an ERP practice that challenged her fears. She learns that she can face uncertainty about contamination and handle the discomfort that arises from her fears.

This is how an initial ERP practice might go. You can see how preparing before ERP practices pays off. Kim clearly got it. She knew what she needed to do: she needed to fully confront her fears and not avoid them. I repeatedly checked in with Kim, and I let her set the pace. When I asked her if she was ready to take the next step and touch the form with her whole hand, she could have said no and chosen to sit with the discomfort she was already feeling for a while longer.

Where would we go from here? I'd ask Kim. She might have an idea, and I'd want to hear it. I might offer suggestions too. We could repeat this practice with other forms. Kim might feel ready to practice holding forms with both hands. She might decide to let the forms touch items that she'll take home with her. Depending on how much we accomplish, she might also touch my desk.

Kim's next step is to plan for response prevention when she leaves the office and to design her homework practices. We want to build on the great work she did in session. She might take forms home with her. We would also discuss how long she will postpone cleaning her hands and changing her clothes after she leaves the office. We'd plan her ERP homework in detail. If the homework is vague, Kim might feel confused and not know what to practice. In addition, we'd plan for obstacles that Kim thinks might interfere with successfully completing her homework on her own.

Sammy: ERP for Responsibility Obsessions

Sammy suffers from the responsibility subtype of OCD. He feels distressed when he thinks about possibly being responsible for anything bad happening to his home and family. His compulsions involve checking household items before leaving home, and his extensive morning ritual interferes with getting out of the house and making it to work on time.

PLANNING ERP FOR RESPONSIBILITY OBSESSIONS

Sammy's hierarchy indicates that although there are many steps in his morning checking ritual, they vary widely in importance. At this point, early in treatment, Sammy feels that completely eliminating all of his morning checking rituals will seem too overwhelming. He isn't sure he can successfully practice not checking the stove, which he rated at 45, or not checking the front door lock, which he rated at 55. These would be challenging practices by themselves, let alone combined with many other practices. Sammy might decide to start by not checking the refrigerator door to be sure that it's closed, which he rated at 10 because the potential consequences don't seem so bad; at worst, food might spoil. Sammy thinks other early practices might include not checking that bathroom faucets are turned off (rated 15) and not checking that small kitchen appliances are unplugged (rated 20)—with the exception of the coffeemaker, which he rated at 30 because he uses it almost every morning and fears there's a higher chance he might leave it on.

Sammy knows that tolerating uncertainty and doubt has to be at the heart of his ERP practices. He also knows that he must challenge how he responds to an inflated sense of responsibility and overestimation of threat. He's currently trapped in a quest for certainty that everything is safe before he leaves home and that he won't be responsible for dangers such as a house fire or burglary. His long-term goal is to tolerate uncertainty and not engage in any checking rituals before leaving the house. We agree that he needs to commit to not returning home to check for reassurance. Instead, he has to learn that he can ride out feelings of anxiety, even if they increase when he leaves the house without completing his checking rituals. In addition, we also discuss the importance of being careful not to mentally check for reassurance throughout the day, since this also feeds the OCD cycle.

Because Sammy has performed his morning checking rituals for so many years, it's probably going to feel difficult to change his behaviors. Even though we decide to break down stopping his morning checking routine into manageable practices, the disruption is likely to make him feel quite anxious. For Sammy to fully lean in, he needs to tolerate the discomfort of taking some risk. He can't "cheat" by staring or even glancing at household items before leaving, because that might give him some reassurance. He needs to fully entertain the possibility that the refrigerator door could be open, that water could be running from a faucet, or that a small appliance could still be plugged in.

Sometimes I travel to clients' homes or other settings to help them start more difficult ERP practices that can't take place in my office, but this isn't always feasible, especially with morning checking routines before going to work. Since most of Sammy's ERP practices will take place outside of my office, we spend much of the session designing a detailed plan for Sammy to practice at home. Because I won't be with him when he practices response prevention during his morning routine, it will be especially important to prepare him for how he might feel and for the obstacles he might encounter.

STARTING ERP FOR RESPONSIBILITY OBSESSIONS

Sammy and I work together to decide exactly what his ERP practice will entail. I ask him to tell me the details about how he checks the refrigerator door. He says, "That's the first thing I check. I pull on the handle to be sure it's closed. Actually, I pull hard enough to open it so I can be sure I close it again. Then I pull just slightly to be sure it doesn't open with a little tug. Sometimes I do the same thing with the door. I stand there long enough to get it to register that the door closed."

When I ask Sammy how long he stands in front of the refrigerator, he says, "I stand there and count to five slowly. I guess I figured out at some point that if I don't see the door open after I stand there for five seconds, it's probably closed." When I ask if he does anything else, he says, "Sometimes—well most of the time—I still have a nagging doubt, so I pull on the refrigerator door again. I usually repeat the whole routine. I repeat it twice unless I'm feeling extremely anxious that day. Eventually, I walk away from the refrigerator because I know I have so many other things to check, and the time pressure to check everything makes me anxious." I ask Sammy if he ever returns to the refrigerator, and he says, "Sometimes I go back for one final check. Usually by then I'm worn out from checking everything else and anxious about being late for work. Sometimes I just stare at the refrigerator for a few more seconds to be sure it's closed."

As you can see from this short discussion, it's important to pay attention to details when planning ERP practices. Just one item on Sammy's hierarchy, checking the refrigerator door, involves many steps. We'll make a plan for response prevention that seems within reach to Sammy. He may decide that he won't check the refrigerator door at all, or he may choose to modify his ritual to reduce the number of times he checks or the length of time he stares. When Sammy feels ready to refrain from checking the bathroom faucets and whether small appliances are plugged in, we can add those items to his ERP practice, making the decision carefully and collaboratively. Our goal is to increase his uncertainty enough for him to benefit from ERP without being overly ambitious and setting up too much for him to tolerate at once. If he were to feel too fearful and return home to check for reassurance, that would just strengthen his OCD.

Sammy and I also discuss how he'll monitor his practices and track his progress. We'll discuss what he learns from these ERP practices regarding his expectations of what will happen when he doesn't complete his checking rituals, including what he learns about his responsibility beliefs and overestimations of threat and how long he can tolerate feeling uncertain. Depending on when we plan to meet for our next session, Sammy may call me with updates about how his practices are going. That way I can offer support and help if he encounters obstacles.

Jennifer: ERP for Violent Thoughts

Jennifer is plagued by violent thoughts and images that are triggered by many situations in her daily life. Her thoughts make her anxious, and she misinterprets them as important and meaningful. She's terrified that she might act on a thought or image of killing someone, especially someone she loves. Because her violent thoughts and images frighten her, she tries not to have them. Of course, as you learned in earlier chapters, trying not to think certain thoughts only makes them show up more often, and this has certainly been the case for Jennifer. She believes that because she has violent thoughts and because they pop into her head frequently, it means she might be capable of acting on them. She misinterprets her thoughts as meaning that she must be a horrible person.

PLANNING ERP FOR VIOLENT THOUGHTS

For Jennifer, an important part of treatment will be teaching her about thought-action fusion. I explain that having violent thoughts doesn't mean acting on them but that she needs to test that out herself. With this type of OCD, treatment involves not trying to push thoughts and images away. I explain to Jennifer that the goal is to learn what happens when she chooses to tolerate the anxiety and uncertainty associated with the violent thoughts and images she thinks about. Although the treatment rationale makes sense to her, Jennifer dreads the idea of riding out the anxiety that her thoughts and images trigger.

Jennifer might decide to begin ERP by repeatedly saying words that frighten her. She's tried her hardest to avoid words such as "knife," "stab," "murderer," and "killer," but they've continued to appear in news articles, TV shows, books, movies, and conversations. Jennifer estimated that saying these words would lead to a SUDS level between 30 and 35.

Jennifer understands that she needs to target her underlying themes by not trying to control her thoughts, and she wants to break the association between having violent thoughts and the meaning she attaches to them. Together, we decide that during her initial ERP practices, Jennifer will allow herself to fully experience the distress triggered by saying feared and avoided words out loud, and that she'll repeat each word until she learns she can tolerate the distress.

Fully leaning in toward aggressive obsessions can be one of the hardest challenges to face. Developing a willingness to face these thoughts and images takes a lot of courage, but it's crucial for treatment to be effective. Jennifer has feared her thoughts for so long that she doesn't have much faith in her ability to begin ERP on her own, so we decide that therapist-assisted practices will be most beneficial at the outset.

STARTING ERP FOR VIOLENT THOUGHTS

First, I check with Jennifer to be sure she's ready to begin. When she's ready, Jennifer starts the practice by repeating the word "knife" out loud. After a few repetitions, she says her anxiety level started at about 50 but is going down. After a few more moments, she says she's feeling more distressed again. When I ask her why she thinks that happened, she says, "I'm imagining knives now when I say the word 'knife.' I see all sorts of kitchen knives and butcher knives. I imagine them with blood on them." I ask her if she can stay with those images and keep repeating the word "knife." She's up for the challenge and repeats, "knife, knife, knife," for several moments. Then she tells me, "It's starting to sound weird." I ask Jennifer if she's still able to hold the images of knives in her mind, and she tells me about the images in vivid detail. Soon she says, "It's not feeling so bad now. It feels a little scary, but it's getting a little boring."

Because Jennifer is doing a great job, I ask if she's ready to take next step on her hierarchy, saying the words "stab," "murderer," and "killer." Jennifer repeats each of these words and, as she does so, allows frightening images to enter her mind. Again, her anxiety increasingly dissipates the longer she practices. Jennifer feels relieved as she learns that her anxiety actually decreases as she accepts frightening words and images. She learns that she can say and think about frightening words and images without disastrous consequences. She changes some of her expectations about thought-action fusion, and she learns that she can handle the distress that disturbing thoughts and images provoke.

Jennifer may feel a great deal of relief and hope after her first ERP session, but she'll need to continue practicing ERP and facing her fears. I'll ask Jennifer if she can repeat this exercise on her own at home. When she's ready to take that step, we'll work together to make a specific plan for when, where, and how long she'll practice and how she can monitor her practices and progress. We might develop creative ideas for homework practices, such as carrying a piece of paper in her pocket that has the scary words written on it. Whatever plan we choose, we'll find a way for Jennifer to continue practicing ERP after she leaves the office.

Cooper: ERP for Symmetry or "Just Right" Obsessions

Cooper might have a hard time sitting in my office because my books aren't lined up by height, and many items on my shelves aren't symmetrically placed. In a way, Cooper is already practicing ERP just by sitting in my office and tolerating discomfort. We could make that explicit and monitor his levels of distress and changes in his expectations about tolerating discomfort when he sits in a room that isn't arranged just right. Cooper has a long list of "just right" obsessions that interfere with his life. He becomes highly distressed if he makes mistakes when writing reports or if his reports end on odd-numbered pages. He spends countless hours rereading and rewriting e-mails and reports for work, and he misses deadlines as a result. He fears being unable to tolerate the discomfort if he doesn't complete tasks "just right."

PLANNING ERP FOR SYMMETRY OR "JUST RIGHT" OBSESSIONS

Cooper might start ERP by intentionally writing imperfectly on a piece of paper to trigger his urge for exactness and symmetry. We might start by practicing this exercise in my office, where he doesn't feel he has much at stake. No one at work will see what he writes in my office. This might sound like an easy exercise, but when it's time to begin, Cooper may find that it triggers more anxiety than he anticipated.

Cooper needs to challenge the belief that if he doesn't write "just so" or if the page doesn't look "just right," he won't be able to tolerate how uncomfortable he feels. Response prevention will involve not correcting imperfections and instead sitting with discomfort. We'll schedule a long enough session to give Cooper the time he needs to freewrite on several pieces of paper. After practicing in session, he'll probably feel ready to practice at home.

STARTING ERP FOR SYMMETRY OR "JUST RIGHT" OBSESSIONS

Cooper tells me that he dreads the idea of intentionally writing in the very way he has spent so much of his life avoiding. I ask him to tell me why he wants to do this exercise, and he says, "Writing and saying things perfectly doesn't sound like such a bad goal. It feels counterintuitive to mess up and not try to make things perfect. Yet I'm anxious all the time and I'm missing work deadlines. It's getting harder to get everything to line up just right." Cooper tells me that he's overwhelmed by a backlog of e-mails. He avoids answering them because he dreads spending so much time crafting each e-mail perfectly. Cooper agrees that he needs to face the discomfort that he tries so hard to avoid. I point out that trying to do everything "just right" isn't making him comfortable either. He smiles and tells me, "You're right. I've been so anxious and miserable. That's why I called you!" Cooper decides that the benefits of practicing ERP are worth it.

Cooper feels ready to start. He begins by writing sentences skewed toward one the side of the page and intentionally makes mistakes and soon discovers his first obstacle: he has trouble deciding what to write. In addition to trying to write symmetrically on the page and with correct grammar, spelling, and punctuation, Cooper also spends an inordinate amount of time deciding what to write. Since we're just starting ERP and practicing one exposure at a time, Cooper and I pick a straightforward topic: details about his drive to the appointment. He still has to decide what he'll write, but the topic is clear.

As Cooper starts writing, he intentionally crosses out words and writes above and below the lines on the paper. After some time, he tells me it's getting easier to do. I notice that Cooper starts writing more slowly and ask him why. He tells me that he keeps strategizing about how to end his paragraph at a "good" place on the page. This is a different item on his hierarchy—and a good illustration of how ERP items may merges with each other. We may decide to move into this next item and have him end his paragraph on the "wrong" part of the page. However, if Cooper doesn't feel ready to do this yet, we could stop at a "good" place and review what he's just accomplished before planning our next step.

While Cooper writes, he may engage in safety behaviors that I might not notice. He admits that as long as he knows he can throw the paper away when he finishes, he feels less distressed. I tell Cooper that I appreciate his honesty; if he can catch safety behaviors like this, we can figure out how to decrease and eliminate them, allowing him to benefit from ERP more fully. He decides to write imperfectly in his journal in session and then take it home with him, which will prevent him from escaping discomfort by throwing away what he writes. Cooper is learning that he can tolerate imperfections and the discomfort he feels when his writing isn't perfect, symmetrical, and "just so."

For his next step, Cooper might decide to stop what he's writing at a random line on the page. He might intentionally stop writing on an odd-numbered page instead of an even-numbered page. Therapist-assisted practices can jump-start Cooper's treatment, but he'll also need to practice on his own. We'll make a detailed homework plan together. Cooper may decide to continue writing "incorrectly" in his journal every day. When he's ready, he can take on additional homework practices, such as sending me daily e-mails that are nonsensical and end on the "wrong" part of a line.

EXERCISE: Exploring Your Thoughts About Treatment Now

In this chapter, you've learned a lot about the early stages of ERP. Hopefully, understanding that you can break ERP into manageable practices has helped decrease your fears about starting treatment. Given everything you've learned, does starting ERP seem more or less frightening than you had imagined? Does it seem more manageable than you expected it would be? Did you read anything that concerns you or raises more questions about ERP? If so, write your concerns and questions in your journal so you can discuss them when you meet with a therapist.

Perhaps you already have some ideas about how you might break down your ERP approach into manageable steps. If so, record your ideas in your journal. If you don't, that's fine; your therapist will help you with this.

Summary

In your initial treatment sessions, you'll discuss your symptoms with your therapist, and then the two of you will probably make a plan for you to monitor your obsessions, compulsions, avoidance behaviors, and the situations that trigger them. You'll develop a game plan to tailor ERP to your particular obsessions and compulsions and the themes underlying them. You'll choose triggers and obsessions to face. You'll set response prevention goals and identify your expectations about the feared consequences of facing your fears and changing your response. You'll also strategize about how you can more fully lean in toward obsessions without using safety behaviors, and decide when to do therapist-assisted practices and when and how to practice on your own.

As the examples in this chapter illustrate, starting ERP may not be as overwhelming as you imagine. Committing to ERP may sound frightening, but with your therapist's help, you'll learn to design initial practices that are achievable. You'll also receive guidance and support from someone who understands your thoughts and fears, and you won't be alone in this process. Once you know that you can tolerate obsessions and the anxiety and distress they trigger without using compulsions, you'll be well equipped to face increasingly challenging situations at various levels of anxiety.

In chapter 6, I'll discuss strategies for creatively leaning in toward obsessions, facing your most challenging fears, practicing imaginal exposures, and handling spontaneous triggers of obsessions. I'll also share how Mary, Gina, and Ted faced some of their most challenging ERP practices.

CHAPTER 6

PUTTING EXPOSURE AND RESPONSE PREVENTION INTO ACTION

Hopefully, what you've learned about initial ERP practices has taken some of the mystery out of starting treatment. Getting started may be more manageable and less frightening than you'd imagined. Still, you know that you'll eventually have to face much more challenging practices if you're going to reach your treatment goals. As you continue to practice and face increasingly distressing thoughts and situations, response prevention can become more difficult. It may be hard to imagine allowing some of your most frightening and disturbing thoughts or images to stay in your mind, rather than trying to suppress them, engaging in compulsions, or seeking reassurance. You probably wonder what it will be like to intentionally face your most anxiety-provoking fears. You may question how you can face your fears about unknown outcomes in the past or future. It can feel overwhelming to think about applying response prevention to the countless spontaneous triggers that could arise every day.

In this chapter, you'll find ideas about how to creatively practice ERP and lean in toward your fears. You'll learn how to face some of your most distressing thoughts and read details on how to practice imaginal exposures to feared scenarios. You'll also learn how to handle spontaneous triggers—now and for the rest of your life.

Strategies for Leaning In Toward Fears

Since the content of obsessions varies, strategies for facing them will vary too. However, there is a unifying thread: accepting and even leaning in toward the content of obsessions, whatever it may be. As mentioned earlier, Mary's therapist used the metaphor of leaning in toward obsessions, and Mary found that language quite helpful:

> Since my obsessions were primarily image based, I needed to focus on exposing my mind to an image and holding the image in my mind in various ways. It sounded scary to hold on to any image or thought that I was so conditioned to try to avoid. But as my therapist explained, the harder you try to *not* think a thought, the stronger and stickier it becomes. Trying not to think about a thought is like straining against a leash. You want to run away from the thought because you fear that you can't take the anxiety that goes with it. By leaning in toward the thought and trying to stay with it, the thought actually weakens. Anxiety can only go so far.

"Leaning in" is a great term to describe ERP. As you know, trying to suppress or avoid thoughts feeds the OCD cycle. Leaning in, as a move in the opposite direction, breaks the cycle. It's fundamentally incompatible with engaging in compulsions and avoidance to alleviate distress. The more you practicing leaning in toward obsessions, the less hold they'll have on you. It may be that the concept makes good sense, but you still wonder what leaning in will look like for you. The short answer is that it will look like whatever your obsessive thoughts and images look like.

Mary's therapist taught her to use creative strategies to accept her thoughts and images and lean in toward them, strategies such as making cartoons of them and talking to them. These strategies gave Mary an approach to facing images that frightened her and made her want to wash. With the guidance of her therapist, Mary practiced leaning in toward thoughts and images that disturbed her. She practiced outside of sessions when she was triggered by people, places, or things that seemed disgusting or indistinguishable to her. Because she practiced in response to spontaneous triggers, her approach to ERP was somewhat fluid. Here's Mary's description of an OCD trigger that she encountered by chance and how she practiced leaning in on her own:

> I went to a Thai restaurant and after (thankfully) finishing the meal, I noticed two long pieces of flypaper hanging from the ceiling. I thought, "Why would a restaurant have dead flies hanging in full view above where people are eating?" It was beyond me, way beyond! I had a lot of anxiety after seeing those yellow-gold sticky flypaper things with tons of dead flies all over them, and I walked closer to them to make sure I was seeing right. I continued to feel anxious and use my same old approach of sorting it out in my head to make sense of what I saw, but to no avail.
>
> Then I decided to start leaning in toward the image. As I walked to my car, I practiced keeping the image in my head. I continued to hold on to the image as much as I could. I woke up four times during the night, and each time I did the same thing, keeping the image in my mind as long as possible. The next day the image was still there, but my anxiety was subsiding—and the image was subsiding too. The epiphany I had with this OCD incident was that for a brief moment, almost like a flash, I felt the total ridiculousness of the whole situation: being so afraid of the image of the flypaper. This was a major source of relief and a sign of progress! So I hung on to that moment of the ridiculousness while continuing to keep the image of the flypaper in my mind.
>
> My therapist told me, "You've got the right idea in staying with the image. The flash of ridiculous is just what you want. It highlights that this is indeed just an image, not a threat. To speed up this effect, you can alter the image a bit, imagining the flies talking to each other or picturing little tombstones on the

strip. Try to stick with exposure to the images, since images are a big trigger for you. You might even try to draw the things you see." So I did that. I drew cartoonlike doodles of the flypaper and the flies chattering amongst themselves. This is what I call a "fast-forward lean in." It really diminished the obsession's hold on me more quickly.

As Mary's flypaper incident illustrates, breaking the OCD cycle involves leaning in toward thoughts and images instead of trying to push them away. Mary gave me many examples of ways she creatively leaned in toward troubling images. One day she saw a small mound of something brownish green on the street and couldn't distinguish what it was. She feared the worst, which caused her to feel contaminated. She wanted to go home and shower, but instead she stayed there and looked at the substance. She imagined taking it for a walk on a leash, and also imagined rubbing it all over her face. As she went about her day, she continued to imagine talking to it. Strategies such as these are used in acceptance and commitment therapy to change the way you interact with your thoughts.

Accepting thoughts and images probably feels counterintuitive, but it's the key to breaking the grip of OCD. The more you practice leaning in toward thoughts and images, the more natural it becomes. Mary told me, "Leaning in was something I practiced continually whenever anything that spiked my anxiety came up. That was the main formula for me: concentrating on it as much as possible instead of running from it. My confidence grew as I learned to accept my thoughts and images more and had less worry about facing new places that might trigger them." Consistently choosing to lean in helped Mary overcome OCD.

Once you understand the concept of leaning in, you have an essential tool for practicing ERP. When underlying OCD themes bring up intense feelings of anxiety, you lean in toward your feared thoughts and images and accept them instead of using compulsions to avoid discomfort. The more you experience the benefit from fully leaning in toward your fears, the more ready you'll feel to face other ERP practices.

Mary's homework practices included intentionally walking on the "icky" side of the street (in her case, the side with more garbage, homeless people, or anything indistinguishable), driving down streets she'd been avoiding, using restaurant restrooms, and visiting friends' homes. Mary returned to places that had previously spiked her OCD, and instead of trying to avoid thoughts and images, she intentionally practiced holding them in her mind. She stayed in situations until her anxiety began to subside, and she intentionally held on to feared images after she left people and places that triggered them. The more she practiced, the more confident she felt about facing other situations.

Facing Your Most Challenging Obsessions

In chapter 5 you saw what initial ERP practices might look like when you break down ERP into manageable steps and start with items that provoke less anxiety. Eventually, you'll need to fully face even the highest items on your hierarchy. Most of my clients have great success during initial ERP practices and feel motivated to take on more situations, but as the practices get more difficult, they're tempted to hold back from facing their most distressing thoughts or situations. This is one reason why a staggered approach to facing items on your hierarchy can be helpful. Once treatment is successfully underway, clients often ask, "Why do I need to face all of the items on my hierarchy? I'm doing so much better. Why can't I stop here?" The answer is that if you avoid facing feared thoughts and images, especially the ones that frighten you the most, you'll start reinforcing the OCD cycle again. You'll strengthen beliefs that you can't handle the discomfort associated with uncertainty, not feeling "just right," or having threatening thoughts and images. If you reinforce avoidance, OCD will still have a hold on you. It makes good sense to eventually practice leaning in toward all intrusive thoughts and images that frighten you, no matter what the content and no matter how anxiety provoking they are. Right now, doing this may seem out of reach, but once you start treatment it should feel more doable.

One of Gina's most dreaded intrusive thoughts involved facing uncertainty about whether she was capable of drowning her baby while bathing her. She was terrified that having such an image and thought meant she might be capable of doing it. The more she avoided giving her baby a bath while home alone with her, the worse her anxiety became. Gina told me how she worked up the courage to face her most challenging and frightening obsession:

My determination to beat OCD began to waver as I started the water for what I told myself was "it": the bath in which I would fully face my fear without resorting to reassurance, no matter how strong and seemingly real my thoughts became. The adrenaline pumping through my body started yelling for me to flee this potentially deadly situation. I fought back by reminding myself that this wasn't for me, but for my precious baby girl, who needed me to be well. I was terrified as I looked down at her cute, chubby little body, wondering if allowing the thoughts would cause me to act on them. Doubt began to consume me. *Would I be capable of doing this homework assignment? Who does something like this for homework, and what if...?* I cried inside, but I forced a smile. I didn't want my baby to sense my distress. "Are you ready for your bath, sweetie? Mommy loves you!" I said as I rubbed her bald little head.

With my heart racing, I checked the water level and temperature. I knew that to do this homework assignment right, the sink had to be filled with an appropriate amount of water, making the possibility of drowning my baby girl real. If I didn't fill it high enough, I'd use the water level to reassure myself that it would be impossible for me to carry through with the act, which would reduce my anxiety, preventing me from fully experiencing the peak of my anxiety. When I saw that the water was high enough, I dipped my hand in to test the temperature. It's sort of ironic to think I was paralyzed by the fear of intentionally harming my child, yet I was concerned about making sure the water wasn't hot enough to burn her.

Nervously, I turned the faucet off. Looking down at the clear bathwater, I felt my chest begin to tighten. I was sick to my stomach, consumed with anxiety, and ripped apart by fear that the nightmare I had been living might become reality in a matter of moments. A barrage of questions fired rapidly through my mind: *What if this isn't OCD? What if I actually do it? My husband will be so devastated when he walks in and sees his lifeless baby girl. Will I take my own life or spend the rest of it in prison? How can I have such thoughts? I must be truly evil!*

Our 1950s-style kitchen, designed to add warmth and happiness through its cheery yellow and green tile counters and matching wallpaper, had become my own personal hell. With my heart in my stomach, I gently laid my daughter down on the bath sling that kept her head above water. My anxiety, already high, began to escalate even more. Trembling, I grasped the counter as if bracing myself for the bad thoughts that were already beginning to flood my mind. Bound and determined, I fought the urge to counter the murderous thoughts with reassuring statements. Instead, with the strength I had prayed for, I forced myself to welcome the thoughts. With my daughter slapping her palms against the water and giggling up at me, my mind swirled with thoughts: *I'm going to drown my daughter right now. This is it. I'm going to do it, and no one is here to stop me.*

My anxiety climbed to a point I didn't know was humanly possible. My ears were burning and my knees felt like they were going to buckle at any moment. I felt that it was only a matter of seconds before I would succumb to my madness. Physically and emotionally weak, I began tickling my daughter's stomach and talking to her while my head spun and my anxiety climbed even further. I didn't know if I could take it much longer. Growing weaker and feeling as though I could faint, I rested my elbows on the counter. Right then, when I thought I couldn't take it any longer, my anxiety peaked and then started dropping rapidly. It was the strangest feeling. I no longer felt as if I was going to pass out. My heart slowed and my mind became clear. With this clarity came a new interpretation of the thoughts that only moments earlier had bound me with paralyzing fear.

The thoughts were still there, but they didn't have the same meaning they held before. They no longer terrified me. In fact, as I stood there watching my daughter, who was happy as could be and completely unaware of what had transpired, they began to feel ridiculous. I rose from the counter trying to comprehend what had just happened. Although just moments before I genuinely feared that I might actually take my daughter's life, I couldn't even conjure up the fear. Still in disbelief, I tried to force the "bad" thoughts into my mind to see if they were truly gone. As hard as I tried, I couldn't get the thoughts to stick. For the first time, they actually seemed to be just what they were: meaningless thoughts and not some dark secret desire.

I had just faced my greatest fear. For the first time, I looked at my baby girl without the burden of wondering whether my thoughts meant I could harm her. The joy I felt cannot adequately be put into words. I had longed to look at my daughter like this since the day she was born: with love unclouded by fear.

Gina's description of completing the most frightening item on her ERP hierarchy beautifully captures all of the elements of successful ERP. She knew that to overcome OCD she needed to give her baby a bath while the two of them were at home alone. She had to fully accept the frightening thoughts that she desperately didn't want to have and the uncertainty and anxiety they provoked. She knew she needed to fully lean in toward her fears and to not use a multitude of safety behaviors, such as bathing her daughter when her husband was home, keeping the bathwater low, or countering her anxious thoughts with reassuring statements. Her therapist couldn't be with her at this stage of her treatment.

If you struggle with this type of OCD, you know how much courage it took for Gina to do this practice. Successfully completing this ERP session was a huge turning point for her. However, even though Gina achieved great success and felt her anxiety diminish, her treatment wasn't finished. She needed to keep giving her baby baths and to face other challenges that arose when aggressive obsessive thoughts led to anxiety and urges to seek reassurance or engage in avoidance.

Imaginal Exposures to Feared Scenarios

Sometimes intrusive thoughts trigger anxiety about possible outcomes that we can never feel sure about in real life. For example, Ted agonized over uncertainty about whether he had made mistakes when performing baptisms, marriages, and last rites. His doubts caused him great anguish decades after he'd performed those priestly duties, but he had no way to achieve certainty about his previous actions or their potential consequences. He had similar difficulties in regard to other aspects of his life, as well. Although many years had passed since certain incidents, he continued to have intrusive thoughts about whether others might have been harmed or someday could be harmed because of his actions: a report he didn't make, a piece of glass he hadn't seen, an abandoned refrigerator he might have missed, or a protruding nail he didn't notice. And incidents that brought up these types of concerns continued to accumulate. Walking down the street could trigger new doubts about possibly seeing broken glass, smelling a gas leak, or missing an object that could cause harm to others.

In Ted's struggle with uncertainty about possibly being responsible for harm coming to others, he can never know for sure whether his fears have been or will be realized. You may suffer from similar themes but with different content. Perhaps you spend countless hours reviewing situations in your head searching for certainty that you're a good person or that you did the right thing. You may repeatedly seek reassurance that you weren't exposed to a sexually transmitted disease. But no matter how many times you convince your doctor to repeat blood tests, you may still question if the results are accurate and whether someday you'll learn the awful truth that you'll die of a dreaded disease and that you unknowingly passed it to others. You may agonize about how to find certainty that your actions will never cause harm to others someday. You probably wonder how to practice ERP with these thoughts. You can still practice ERP, but you'll need to use imaginal exposure, facing feared scenarios in your imagination.

Ted's Experience of Imaginal Exposure

If you look at Ted's initial exposure hierarchy in chapter 3, you'll notice that most of his exposure items involved intrusive thoughts about events that occurred in the past, sometimes years ago. His uncertainty about past events was a source of great anguish. With his therapist's guidance, Ted wrote scripts of his feared scenarios. While writing them, he didn't seek reassurance; instead, he faced his fears and leaned in toward dreaded thoughts and images. He also wrote imaginal scripts about current scenarios and doubts that helped him learn to lean in toward those fears. When you write imaginal scripts, you intentionally think about dreaded thoughts and images that you've been trying to avoid or suppress. You can either make an audio recording of your script to listen to it repeatedly or simply reread it again and again. As a next step, you can then write new and more detailed scripts of the feared scenario and repeat those. With this repeated exposure, you'll learn that you can face your fears and the discomfort those thoughts and images provoke.

Ted wrote a script about being responsible for airline disasters because of something he'd overheard but not reported many years before. He wrote about the situation that initially triggered his obsession and his fears about what could happen if he tried to correct his oversight today. As he wrote, his SUDs level rose to 80. Then he made an audio recording of what he'd written. As he repeatedly listened to his recording, he was increasingly able to lean in toward his fears. Here's Ted's script about being responsible for airline disasters:

> *I was investigating a discrimination case at an airline factory. While I was on-site, a disgruntled employee complained that his supervisor made him patch up bad welds. I thought, That could lead to a disaster. Even though I was investigating a discrimination case, I did have a form that I could have used to relay the information to the appropriate department, but I didn't do it. Years passed, and I never reported it. Horrible accidents could happen on planes built there.*
>
> *I'm responsible for airline disasters because I didn't send in a report. I'm responsible for hundreds of people dying. If just one*

guy—me—had reported it, airline disasters wouldn't have happened. I could have reported it. Because I didn't, lots of people died. People are afraid to fly because of me.

Finally, I report it to the FAA. When I tell them, I'm immediately handcuffed and dragged off to jail. I'm humiliated. There are big headlines in the paper saying that I'm responsible for airline crashes. Barbara, my wife, gets hateful phone calls from her friends, reacting to me, her cowardly husband. If I had filed a report in 1975, none of this would have happened. Hundreds of people died because of me. Every bad weld on planes at that factory was my fault.

Ted described how he felt when he started listening to his audio recording:

I felt really anxious and started questioning whether this was just my excessive anxiousness. I don't want to be responsible for all of the deaths that might have occurred or may occur in the future. I don't want to live with this feeling. I don't want this to haunt me. I don't want this to lie heavy on my conscience on my deathbed, to know that even after I'm gone people will die because of me. All of those thoughts flooded my mind as I started listening. My discomfort was at the level of sweating!

I listened to the recording over and over. By the tenth time, my distress had gone way down. I felt much calmer as I listened. Just listening over and over again has this effect. I heard the words, but they didn't seem so loaded anymore. And by the sixteenth or twentieth time, different thoughts began to come into my mind, like *I generally make good decisions. My decision at the time made good sense.* I wasn't trying to reassure myself anymore. I genuinely began to see things from a different perspective. I wasn't certain about that one decision, but I was calmer. Although I never lowered my SUDS level to a zero, I began to see my thoughts in a different light.

Ted's script captures many components of ERP: remembering the day he overheard that employee talk about bad welds instead of trying to suppress the memory; facing his fear of being irresponsible instead of trying to seek reassurance that nothing had gone wrong; and facing his feared consequences of what could happen if he made a report now. His script also follows a key guideline for imaginal exposure: it's important to write scenarios that allow you to face your fears head-on without using safety behaviors to keep a distance from them. Ted's script elicited a great deal of anxiety, but he was able to persist in listening to it. His anxiety never completely diminished, but he learned that he could face his fears and tolerate how that made him feel. In fact, he learned that his distress actually decreased and that he didn't need to avoid thoughts about this incident.

Once you listen to or read a script repeatedly and your SUDS level lowers, it's tempting to think that you're done with that fear once and for all. The truth is, those doubts may intrude at any time, but because of your experience with imaginal exposure, you'll know how to lean in toward them. Here's how Ted described this:

> As I worked on the plane scenario, I brought my SUDS down to a low level, so I thought I was done with it. But at various times those thoughts would come up and trigger my anxiety again. So I wrote up a new script, recorded it on my digital recorder, and listened to it, just as I did when I first practiced. Still, thoughts about planes crashing came to me at inconvenient times, so I also used a couple of other strategies to face my fears. One was to take ten or fifteen minutes to repeatedly write words such as "bad welds" and "fatal crash." Another was to concentrate on the feeling of being responsible for doing something wrong. I recalled the airline factors. I thought about how I failed. I thought, *If you had done one thing, everything would have been solved.* Eventually it started to sound ridiculous again and I knew I could handle the uncertainty I felt.

Writing imaginal scripts allows you to lean in toward any and all possible consequences that you fear. You can be as creative as possible when you vividly create scenarios in your imagination. Although fully facing your fears will feel distressing at first, you can finally break the OCD cycle by leaning in toward fears in your imagination. Most importantly, you'll have a tool to use whenever your anxiety or discomfort spikes due to an obsession: lean in toward your fears in your imagination.

Designing Imaginal Exposures

Like Gina, many people with aggressive intrusive thoughts fear losing control and hurting or murdering someone, often a loved one. If you have similar frightening thoughts, you could write a script that involves killing your loved one, going to jail, being separated from everyone you love, and dying in prison. You might imagine how surprised everyone is to learn that you're a murderer and include details such as hearing what your friends and neighbors say about you. You could also include the idea that your therapist was wrong about you and didn't see that you were capable of committing a horrendous act. This may sound extreme, but the goal of imaginal exposure is the same as in real-life exposure and response prevention: facing feared thoughts and images, fully leaning in toward them, and not seeking safety by avoiding the fears that frighten you the most. If you realize that you're leaving out important details, try to go the distance and imagine everything you fear but have been trying not to think.

One of the greatest fears that many people with OCD face is living the rest of their life with uncertainty. Imaginal exposure allows you to intentionally face that fear too. For example, you can write about how it might feel to live your life never knowing for certain that your intentions are pure and that you always act with integrity. You might write about developing a horrible disease someday and never knowing if it was because of something you touched today, a scenario that might involve ongoing uncertainty that your blood test results are accurate. Imaginal exposure to living life with uncertainty is a form of leaning in.

Your therapist can help you create imaginary scenarios and plan how and when to practice. Together, you'll discuss how you can face intrusive thoughts and images without seeking reassurance, using compulsions, or subtly trying to avoid them. Imaginal exposure can also be a great way to practice an ERP exercise before facing it in real life. For example, if it feels too hard to leave your home without completing a checking routine, you can practice doing it in your imagination first.

Combining Imaginal and Real-Life Exposure

Another possibility is combining imaginal scripts with real-life practices. If you fear intrusive thoughts about being capable of harming children, you might record a scenario of becoming a child molester and rotting in prison forever, and then listen to the recording while walking in a park full of children. If you fear blasphemous thoughts, you might record blasphemous scenarios and listen to them daily while viewing photos of religious figures.

Ted took this approach with his fears about not removing all fragments of broken glass in parks and on sidewalks and being responsible if someone stepped on them. He made a recording about these fears, including his greatest fear: being tormented forever by having allowed harm to come to others. Then he repeatedly listened to the recording while walking in parks and along sidewalks and *not* scanning for glass to pick up. Here's the script he recorded:

I'm in the park. It's the kind of day for a picnic. I'm walking across the grass, and I spot some glass fragments in the grass. I immediately go over and see pieces of a broken bottle. There are four larger pieces sticking up, with knifelike points that appear to be extremely sharp, and the points are in a vertical position. They definitely have to be picked up. Someone could easily not notice them and step right on them with bare feet. A guy receiving a football pass could come right down on them, and they could dig into his foot and tear it for three to four inches. A baby learning to walk could step on them and sever her foot almost in half, or she could fall on them and cut her thigh, causing a gushing of blood and requiring immediate emergency care.

I'll definitely pick up the main pieces, but there may be other glass fragments that aren't so prominent. They could easily be hidden in the grass and end up cutting a teenager's foot as he chases his girlfriend. Even though I pick up the larger pieces, I miss the smaller remnants that remain hidden. For a little girl or boy who's unaware of them, they're almost as treacherous as the big pieces I picked up. A child will step right on the glass, and a tiny bit will lodge under her skin. The big splinters would probably cause a victim to need stitches. The little chips would be painful to dig out, and the child's parents might even say, "I can't see anything there."

I'm responsible to take care of this danger! If I don't find all of the glass fragments, I'll feel guilty for allowing someone to be injured or for causing considerable pain to someone. If I walk by, I'll experience a gnawing guilt, and I'll think about it when I go to bed at night. I'll sleep erratically, if at all. If the harm is serious enough, it will be a mortal sin and I'll suffer in hell forever. I'll always feel guilty.

Ted needed to decide what to do if he saw large glass fragments. Although he tried not to look for them, it was inevitable that he would find some in spite of his best efforts. His ERP plan was to not pick them up; yet, as Ted's therapist explained, there could be times when it would be important to take action. Ted struggled with how arbitrary this plan sounded. Yet as he practiced, he learned that he could resist picking up pieces of glass when they were just fragments lying in picnic areas. But once when he saw a large, protruding piece of glass, he chose to move it. Ted still struggles when deciding whether a trigger presents imminent or remote danger, but he has learned that resisting his urges doesn't result in going too far in the other direction and becoming an irresponsible person. Instead, he's learned that he can feel anxious and not pick up every nail or piece of glass that he sees.

EXERCISE: Identifying Your Ideas for ERP Practices

Now that you know more about the range of what ERP practices can look like—both in real life and using imaginal exposure—you may have ideas about what types of practices could be most beneficial for you. Write your ideas in your journal. Also be sure to write any questions you may have so that you can discuss them with your therapist.

Did the examples in this chapter give you any ideas about how you might lean in toward your fears and break the OCD cycle? For example,

Mary used creative strategies to hold dreaded images in her head while she practiced response prevention. Can you think of any creative strategies you might use to lean in toward your fears?

You probably can relate to how Gina felt as she practiced ERP with the highest item on her hierarchy. You may feel motivated to work with a therapist to confront your greatest OCD fears, or you may have concerns about practicing a similar ERP exercise. If you have concerns, write them in your journal. If you have ideas about how to face your greatest fears, write those down too.

Do you think imaginal exposure might help you face your fears? You may have ideas for imaginal scenarios that can help you practice ERP. If it feels manageable, try writing some notes about your ideas. If it feels too distressing, you need not write about this now. Your therapist will talk with you about ideas for ERP, including imaginal exposures, when you're ready.

Handling Spontaneous Triggers of Obsessions

Although you may start treatment by practicing ERP in planned scenarios with known triggers, inevitably you'll encounter spontaneous triggers of obsessions and experience urges to engage in compulsions. When that happens, you'll probably think, *Wait! This situation can't happen yet. I'm not ready for it!* For example, while you're working on exposure to contamination fears, something out of the blue could trigger a new contamination fear. Perhaps some unknown substance falls on your car, a red spot appears on your clothing, or you spot a syringe in the grass as you walk down the sidewalk. New contamination triggers lurk around every corner and can activate new fears. Life doesn't follow a well-planned exposure hierarchy, so learning to handle various levels of distress across multiple situations will be important. You can decide in advance what to do when you encounter triggers that spike your anxiety but that you hadn't planned to tackle yet.

Your therapist will help you decide how to handle spontaneous triggers, and your plan will probably change over time as you become more skilled at leaning in toward thoughts and images that trigger discomfort and urges to use compulsions. Ultimately, you want to face any obsession or situation, at any level of distress, without using compulsions. But because this goal may feel too overwhelming during early stages of treatment, you can devise plans to break down spontaneous ERP practices into small steps, allowing you to continue to make progress by not fully engaging in compulsions. Of course, the more you practice leaning in toward obsessions and refraining from using compulsions, the more quickly you'll reach your treatment goals.

Mary never knew what triggers lay in wait for her or how anxiety provoking they might be. Almost any person, item, or place could trigger her anxiety and compulsions to wash away dreaded images and feelings. Mary changed her responses to these spontaneous triggers gradually, experimenting with postponing washing rituals or only engaging in parts of the rituals. Here's how she described the steps she took when she faced more spontaneous triggers than she felt ready to handle in a day:

One day I parked at a pharmacy and started to walk toward the store. I saw a badly disfigured and unkempt woman waiting at the bus stop. She had a very squished, distorted face, with lots of moles and facial hair. If my friend Wendy had been there, she probably would have said, "Wow, that's a freaky-looking person!" and then walked in. I reacted by immediately turning around and running back toward my car. I wanted to transfer my prescriptions to another pharmacy, but the refill for one prescription was already there. Before I started my car to leave, I tried to breathe and gather my therapy tools. Just the act of staying in the parking lot—not running from my fears—allowed me to feel the panic subside.

I imagined what my therapist would say: "Go back and do what you came here to do. Walk past that person and look at her." I got out of the car. The freaky person was still waiting for the bus. I looked at her and went into the pharmacy. That wasn't easy to do. The hardest things for me to lean in toward are people or things that I'm uncertain about. My mind asks, *What's wrong with this person? Why does she look like that?* What's hardest is the feeling that I need to get the thought off of me.

So for the rest of the day, I continued to try to hold the image of that woman in my head. When I got home, it felt too hard to not wash at all, but hey, baby steps count. So I changed my washing ritual. I allowed myself to shower but not wash my hair.

Mary encountered a spontaneous trigger during a time when she was practicing ERP for multiple other triggers. She made great strides by practicing leaning in toward that spontaneous trigger image, not avoiding the pharmacy, and not engaging in part of her washing ritual. At that point in treatment, Mary wasn't yet able to always refrain entirely from washing.

Ted created imaginal scripts on the spot when he encountered spontaneous triggers of obsessions. He described it like this:

Facing my fears doesn't always mean just facing the physical location of the fear. I can walk by a location and smell natural gas, but my anguish doesn't go away just because I walk past the location over and over again. Response prevention means not mulling over the looming danger. Instead of walking by and doing nothing, I create a narrative of the danger, such as imagining that five houses blow up, eighteen people are killed by the explosion, eight are maimed for life, and husbands, wives, and children are grieving because I didn't do anything about it. That's the kind of narrative that I have to repeat again and again in my mind to diminish the anguish. It's not easy and I don't like it, but it's better than anguishing about my guilt and doubts.

Spontaneous triggers present opportunities to practice ERP when you're caught by surprise. When clients tell me about finding creative ways to lean in toward spontaneous triggers and reduce or eliminate compulsions, I know that they're beginning to own their treatment. Instead of relying on me to offer suggestions, they're experimenting with their own ideas. They're becoming skilled at being their own therapists. We continue to work closely together to plan or practice ERP and devise strategies for handling spontaneous triggers, but they've developed the skills for facing OCD triggers on their own.

Practicing leaning in toward obsessions and using response prevention is a lifelong endeavor. New triggers or obsessions can catch you by surprise, but as long as you practice leaning in toward fears and not using compulsions or avoidance, you can challenge underlying OCD themes no matter what form they take. And each time you use these skills, you'll be reinforcing new responses to OCD triggers.

Recognizing Your Progress

At times, you may feel exhausted from deciding how to handle the spontaneous triggers that come up throughout the day. You might practice leaning in but still feel like you've failed because you didn't completely refrain from engaging in compulsions or using safety behaviors. You might make great strides in planned ERP but feel discouraged when you have difficulty handling spontaneous triggers on your own. One useful strategy is to keep a log of positive steps, both big and small, that you take each day.

A log of positive steps can be helpful in many ways. As you practice what you learn in treatment, it can be easy to lose sight of your progress toward breaking the OCD cycle. Every step counts. Keeping a log of these steps will help you recognize your progress, especially when it doesn't seem obvious. Just as you strengthened the OCD cycle over time by engaging in compulsions, you can strengthen new responses and efforts to break the cycle by logging and reviewing your successes. Still, in spite of your best efforts, you may occasionally get caught in the OCD cycle and feel discouraged. When you think of the work that lies ahead, you may feel that your efforts and successes are only a drop in the bucket. Monitoring your progress will help you remember the great work you've been doing and provide a record of how much you're accomplishing along the way.

EXERCISE: Keeping a Positive Steps Log

By reading this book, you've already taken a positive step toward challenging OCD. Even if you haven't started treatment or contacted a therapist yet, you're learning about OCD and treatment for OCD. If you've been doing the exercises in this book, you've taken other positive steps toward understanding your OCD cycle and preparing for treatment. All of these positive steps are worth recording. I hope you'll give yourself credit for having the courage to take these initial steps toward challenging OCD. If you've taken additional steps such as reading material on the website of the International OCD Foundation or reading other books about OCD, log those as well. Of course, taking concrete actions to find a treatment provider and initiating treatment will be important and necessary positive steps toward achieving the goal of overcoming OCD.

You might want to use a separate notebook or journal for your positive steps log so you can easily review it at any time. Go ahead and record any positive steps you've already taken. Your entries can be very free-form, but it's important to be specific about dates, triggers, obsessions, and the positive steps you've taken to change your responses to obsessions; otherwise it may be hard to remember what you've accomplished. Also, take care in how you log your positive steps. Your goal is to log any new responses to triggers, obsessions, and urges to use compulsions, including responses to old triggers that become problematic again. It can feel discouraging to be challenged by triggers or obsessions you have already faced, but success lies in how you respond to the underlying OCD themes those triggers reflect.

Here are a couple of example entries, the first for someone with contamination obsessions, and the second for someone with repsonsibility obsessions and checking compulsions:

> July 29, 2013. On my way into the shopping mart today, I accidentally brushed up against somebody on the sidewalk and felt really contaminated. I wanted to go home and shower. Instead, I went into the store and bought the items I wanted. I brought them into my house and practiced touching them. I even put them into circulation with other items in my house! I only washed my hands once, even though I wanted to do my washing ritual. I didn't use antibacterial soap.

> November 2, 2013. I left home in a hurry this morning and couldn't remember if I checked the back door lock. I caught myself mentally retracing my footsteps, trying to reassure myself that the door was locked. When I realized what I was doing, I told myself that the door

might be unlocked and that I couldn't know for certain. It made me uncomfortable, but I practiced accepting the uncertainty whenever doubts about the door entered my mind. I didn't go home at lunch to check the door.

Summary

This chapter described many aspects of ERP. As you progress in treatment, you'll apply ERP principles you learn during initial practices to more challenging situations. Successful treatment involves continuing to face feared thoughts and situations while using response prevention. It takes courage to lean in toward distressing thoughts, disturbing images, and uncomfortable feelings. Using creative imagery, as Mary did, can be one way to approach using ERP. Facing your most challenging fears without using safety behaviors can feel extremely frightening but, as Gina's story illustrates, it can yield powerful and life-changing results. Some exposures may require imaginal exposure to feared scenarios and consequences, as many of Ted's practices did. Your therapist will guide you when developing strategies to handle spontaneous triggers of obsessions and urges to engage in compulsions. ERP practices target underlying OCD themes, but your approach will be personalized, addressing your specific obsessions and compulsions. In this chapter, Mary, Gina, and Ted described some of their ERP practices, demonstrating how different treatment can look while still achieving the same goals.

Treatment progress doesn't usually follow a straight line, no matter how well planned the ERP approach is. It's common to hit bumps along the way as you strive to reach your goals. In chapter 7, I'll address common treatment obstacles and offer ideas for overcoming them.

CHAPTER 7

OVERCOMING
OBSTACLES

In earlier chapters, I provided a general outline of how treatment for OCD ideally goes. Of course, treatment doesn't always go as planned. You'll begin by working with your therapist to design a plan that's individualized to fit your symptoms, but even with an individualized plan, it's common to encounter obstacles. In fact, I tell my clients to expect obstacles. At some time or another, everyone hits a bump in the road. It's not shameful to encounter obstacles, and it doesn't mean you're failing in treatment. It's just part of the process—and a learning opportunity. Both clients and therapists learn from what doesn't go according to plan.

When you encounter obstacles, your therapist will help you figure out why. Perhaps some of your ERP practices don't target your core fears. Maybe your homework wasn't well planned. Life stressors can interfere with doing therapy homework. You may hit roadblocks and feel less motivated to continue facing your fears. You might get tired of practicing ERP. These are just a few of the potential pitfalls. By figuring out what's causing the problem, you can better understand your obstacles and come up with solutions. In addition, what you learn can also help you plan for future obstacles or setbacks.

In this chapter, I discuss some of the most common obstacles my clients encounter and offer suggestions for overcoming them. If you've begun treatment, you may already be familiar with some of the obstacles I describe. If you haven't started treatment, knowing about common obstacles can help you plan ahead and be prepared for them. I offer suggestions on how to overcome common obstacles, but your therapist will have ideas too, and you'll have your own ideas. In fact, since you're the expert on your own experience with OCD, you already may be able to predict some of the difficulties that might arise.

Obstacle: Uncertainty About Treatment

As you know, uncertainty is an underlying theme in OCD. So it makes sense that problems with uncertainty about treatment might arise during the course of treatment. It's likely that at some point during treatment you'll question ERP practices, therapy homework, and even treatment itself. Some of those concerns may be valid and worth talking through with your therapist. Often, though, feelings of uncertainty start to hold people back from taking necessary steps toward finishing treatment and achieving their treatment goals. You might get stuck in an OCD cycle of wanting certainty about what you're doing in treatment. You might think, *Until I feel certain that I'm doing the right thing, I'm not willing to risk doing certain ERP practices.* But what you're really saying is *I need to feel certain before I face a fear without using compulsions.* Remember, this is the type of thinking that you're trying to challenge and change. If you avoid the uncomfortable feelings associated with facing uncertainty, you'll slip back into perpetuating the OCD cycle.

Suggestions

Review the rationale for your treatment plan. Old habits are hard to break. You've probably been seeking certainty for a long time. It's understandable that you might seek certainty about treatment too. At the same time, challenging intolerance of uncertainty is the goal of treatment. Breaking free from the grip of OCD requires that you intentionally face uncertainty. Seeking opportunities to tolerate uncertainty is inherently part of treatment. If you wait until you feel certain before moving forward, you may feel stuck for a long time!

To overcome this obstacle, review your responses to the exercises in chapters 3 and 4 about why it's worth it to you to actively engage in this treatment and challenge your underlying OCD themes, especially intolerance of uncertainty. You may want to think through those exercises again and write further thoughts in your journal. For example, you could add new advantages and disadvantages to facing fears that come up during the course of treatment. You might write more details about living life the way you want to live without being at the mercy of compulsions. When clients feel stuck, I often ask them to revisit why they want to learn to accept uncertainty instead of avoid it. Remembering the bigger picture about why you're doing this hard work will help you stay motivated at each step along the way.

Obstacle: Perfectionism

As with intolerance of uncertainty, the underlying OCD theme of perfectionism can interfere with treatment. You may strive to practice ERP "perfectly" and question whether you're doing your homework in just the right way. It's likely that you'll question your treatment progress too. You may wonder, *Am I making progress quickly enough? How do I compare to other people who have done this?* You might compare your treatment plan to what you read in books or hear from others in OCD support groups. In the quest to successfully complete treatment, perfectionism may cause you to feel anxious and question whether you're tolerating discomfort or engaging in response prevention in "just the right way." If part of your OCD has been striving to do everything "just right," there's a good chance you'll bring that ambition into therapy too.

Perfectionism about treatment can sometimes lead to developing new compulsions. It's not uncommon for people with OCD to begin imposing rigid rules on their behaviors in a quest to do ERP perfectly.

For example, you might decide that a new rule is to wash your hands for only one minute or check appliances for just two minutes before leaving the house. These may be steps in the right direction, but if the desire is to have new rules to rely on to be certain you're complying with treatment correctly, these new rules can become fixed and dictate new responses to obsessions. No room is left for flexibility. It may feel like you're doing therapy homework "just right," but reliance on rigid rules about behaviors such as washing, checking, or counting in the quest to be certain you're doing ERP correctly can turn into new compulsions.

Suggestions

Since you know that perfectionism is an underlying OCD theme, be aware that it might creep up in your treatment, just as it did in the development of your symptoms. Awareness is half the battle. Once you're aware that perfectionism is interfering with your treatment, you can challenge it.

View this obstacle as an opportunity. You can creatively lean in toward perfectionism-related fears about your treatment and how you do ERP practices. For example, you can devise homework practices that are more open-ended, forcing you to be more flexible and creative when deciding how to use response prevention on your own. You could plan to wash your hands for varying lengths of time under one minute instead of setting a specified time limit. Likewise, you can practice breaking new, perfectionistic rules and intentionally changing your responses. For example, if you'd had a compulsion to end your reading on even-numbered pages and created a new rule to only end on odd-numbered ones, you could vary where you stop, sometimes on even-numbered pages, other times on odd-numbered pages. You could also apply imaginal exposure to this obstacle, writing a scenario about the consequences of not participating in therapy perfectly. There are many creative methods for breaking out of perfectionism traps. Your therapist can guide you in designing strategies to overcome perfectionism about therapy.

Obstacle: Difficulty Completing Therapy Homework

What sounds like a good homework plan during a session doesn't always feel so great when it comes time to do it. Practicing ERP on your own can be especially challenging. You may have difficulty getting started or completing your intended practices. Even after you become well practiced at ERP, you're likely to encounter this obstacle at some point during treatment. It's common for people to get off track in practicing ERP from time to time.

Reasons for not completing therapy homework can include not being clear about what you're supposed to do, not planning ahead to allow time to practice, or simply avoiding doing it. Sometimes life presents unexpected difficulties. Your child might be home sick, or you might have a bad cold yourself. You may have an upsetting argument with your spouse, need to stay late at work, or feel worn down by multiple stressors during the week. Integrating ERP homework into your daily life can be challenging. And even if you're well practiced at completing your therapy homework, you may get tired of practicing or feel afraid to take a particular step in facing your fears.

Gina ran into difficulty completing her ERP homework when she worked on her first hierarchy, which involved facing doubts about her sexual orientation:

> At each appointment, my therapist encouraged me to take the leap of faith and do ERP as homework. Often, I told him, "No way," or I agreed to do it but had no intention of actually doing what he suggested. My homework consisted of me not resisting my "gay" thoughts and instead embracing them by doing things like watching movies with gay characters and looking at a *Playboy* magazine. I could never complete these homework plans because I feared that I'd come to realize my doubts weren't OCD. I always chickened out before my anxiety could climb and peak out. At one point, my therapist tried to give me what

he thought would be an easier suggestion. He asked me to buy a rainbow gay pride sticker and put it in my bathroom at home. I just looked at him, laughed, and said, "There's no way!" Rainbow stickers could send me into a full-blown panic attack. Because I didn't do the homework, my sexual orientation obsessions continued to haunt me.

Suggestions

If a homework plan feels too overwhelming, decide how to break it into more manageable steps. If you're uncertain about your homework practice, discuss your confusion or questions with your therapist. You may need to make more specific plans about when, where, how long, or how often to practice. You may need help figuring out how to integrate homework into your daily life.

Try to be creative. Life has a way of interfering with homework, no matter how well planned. The more you practice ERP, the more creative you'll become at finding ways to practice even if the day doesn't go according to plan. If your spouse is home sick or you have unexpected visitors, you can still look for opportunities to practice, even though your practice may not be exactly as you'd originally planned. Any step you take toward changing your responses to obsessions and refraining from urges to engage in compulsions is a step in the right direction.

Remember to log your positive steps, no matter how small they may seem. You want to reinforce not only completing your ERP homework, but also becoming more creative and flexible in practicing on your own. It feels good and motivating to see how much you've accomplished, especially when you hit tough times and struggle with completing ERP homework.

In addition, write in your journal about obstacles you encounter in doing ERP homework. You may feel discouraged, alone, tired of practicing, or nervous about taking on your next item. All of these concerns are worth discussing in session. Your therapist may have some suggestions. For example, you might schedule more pleasurable activities to counterbalance the challenges of ERP. You might choose to reward yourself for completing difficult homework practices. You could decide to talk with certain family members or friends to gain more emotional support. You might check in with your therapist more frequently between sessions. There's no need to feel alone and stuck when figuring out how to overcome obstacles to completing ERP homework.

Obstacle: Confusion About Legitimate vs. OCD Concerns

You may have heard people say, "If you have to ask if it's OCD, it probably is." It's common to feel confused about certain feared situations and wonder, *How do I know whether my concerns are legitimate or part of my OCD?* Your habitual response to OCD triggers has been to decide that your fears are worthy of using compulsions or avoidance. But once you embark on treatment, you may not feel sure whether you can trust your own judgment. This gives you another opportunity to choose to accept uncertainty and lean in toward it. Still, sometimes choosing response prevention seems too threatening. You might ask yourself, *What if I'm wrong?* Your choice may become especially challenging if you feel extremely frightened when encountering a spontaneous trigger. You don't want to sabotage your treatment progress, yet you might feel scared, confused, and stuck when deciding what to do. This quandary is similar to one of the fairly common fears people have before starting treatment: *What if I go too far in the other direction and do something that's irresponsible?*

Suggestions

To assess the legitimacy of a concern, consider the frequency and intensity of your thoughts and urges. If your thoughts and fears occur with great frequency or intensity and a strong urgency to do something to relieve distress, this may indicate that you're facing an OCD trigger. Remember, OCD thoughts aren't necessarily different from thoughts that might cross other people's minds, but they can stick and create a sense of threat and urgency. Take a moment to pause and think about how you're interpreting your thoughts and responding to them. Also remember that your goal is to face uncertainty while engaging in response prevention, even if this feels more distressing at first.

Another helpful strategy is to consider what others would do if faced with the same situation. Clients often start to smile when I ask them to consider alternative perspectives. They recognize that most people wouldn't use a compulsion if faced with a similar situation. They also tell me how embarrassed they'd feel if someone knew their reasoning for engaging in a compulsion or saw them doing it. These considerations can help you assess whether a response is being driven by OCD.

Along the same lines, watch what others do in similar situations. For example, you can watch how others handle household items, leave the house, or interact with people whom you might deem to be contaminated. If you're in a relationship with someone who doesn't have OCD, you can watch your significant other to help you determine if your behaviors would seem over-the-top. Ted told me about how he used this strategy:

My wife doesn't have an OCD bone in her body. If we're going for a walk and I see a nail or a piece of glass, I think I should pick it up. She walks right by it. I try to gauge my reactions by hers. I seem to have a syndrome that I'm some kind of messiah and have to save the world because I see things that no one else sees and that have to be corrected. My wife often brings me down to earth. I've learned to restrain myself from asking her for reassurance, but her example often saves the day.

When you're truly unsure about how people without OCD would respond to a situation, you and your therapist might also conduct a survey. Just be aware that this can be a tricky option: you need to take great care not to conduct surveys in order to seek reassurance. Your therapist can be helpful here, providing some guidance in whether a survey might be an appropriate way to learn about how others would respond to a situation that triggers your anxiety and urge to use compulsions or engage in avoidance. You may have used compulsions for so long that you have difficulty seeing how others think and act differently than you do.

Obstacle: Difficulty Recognizing Compulsions

If you've engaged in compulsions and avoidance for a long time, it might be hard to recognize when you do, especially if these behaviors crept up on you over the course of many years. When compulsions become a natural part of your life, it can take a while to distinguish them from more appropriate responses. Here's how Mary described this difficulty:

> The hardest part for me was the actual awareness of when I was avoiding. My instinct to avoid was so ingrained. It would be like driving to the same job for forty years, then getting a new job and finding yourself still driving to the old one. In the begin-ning, there were so many compulsions that I sometimes didn't even know I was doing them. My behaviors were so habitual that I wasn't conscious enough of them to remember to practice leaning in or changing my rituals. I continued to avoid some streets and sidewalks or contact with certain things because doing so had been part of my routine for so long. It was so habit-ual that it took me a while to realize, *Oh, this is also part of my OCD.* For instance, I wouldn't go to a certain laundromat because I'd once found a maxi pad in one of the washers. It took me a few years to finally add that to my list of places to not avoid—not because it had felt too difficult to do, but because it had become so "off the list" that it didn't occur to me that the laundromat was a trigger.

Suggestions

However far into treatment you are when you recognize a compul-sion or avoidance behavior, practice leaning in and changing your response. If you've engaged in OCD behaviors for quite some time, they may seem to make good sense until you see them for what they are. What's important is that you stay on the lookout for compulsions and avoidance behaviors, even subtle ones, and view them as opportunities to practice exposure and response prevention. You're not failing in treatment if you don't recognize all of your compulsions right away. And remember, you don't need to be perfect at therapy or complete everything on your hierarchy on a perfect timeline. Recognizing obsessions and urges to engage in compulsions is a lifelong endeavor, and it will become more automatic the more you practice. What's important is that you change your responses and behaviors when you realize that you're engaging in compulsions or avoidance.

If you miss an opportunity to practice ERP, all is not lost. Mary often returns to places to practice leaning in. You can correct for automatically engaging in a compulsion by entering the situation again and intentionally practicing ERP. There are many ways to practice such do-overs. For example, if you realize that you automatically washed your hands after feeling contaminated, you can go back and touch the same item or similar items that make you feel contaminated and not wash. If you instinctively arranged items perfectly before leaving your desk, you can return to your desk and purposely place them in a disordered pattern. If you avoided reading an article about serial killers because you feared it would trigger unwanted aggressive obsessions, you can return to the article and read it later.

Obstacle: Feeling Like Some Practices Are Too Difficult to Do on Your Own

Even after you become well practiced in ERP, you may find it difficult to muster the courage to complete certain practices on your own. Earlier in this chapter, you read about how Gina had difficulty practicing ERP homework that involved facing doubts about her sexual orientation. She eventually managed to practice looking at women in *Playboy* magazines and watching movies with gay characters in them, but she didn't complete many other homework practices, such as repeatedly listening to a script recorded in her own voice about possibly being gay. After the birth of her daughter, Gina shifted the focus ERP to her harming fears because they interfered with being the mother she wanted to be. In spite of her great success in learning to face her harming fears on her own at home, she continued to struggle with fears related to doubts about being gay—doubts that became more frequent and intense because she hadn't fully faced them. She found practicing ERP for these doubts on her own at home to be too difficult. For several reasons, including the difficulty of these practices, she took a break from treatment and her sexual orientation obsessions intensified.

Ted encountered a similar obstacle in his ERP practices focused on fears of potentially causing harm through "misstatements," like telling people that coffee can be beneficial. When he went home to practice telling his in-laws, "The dangers of too much salt in the diet are overstated," he felt too anxious to do it.

Suggestions

Doing ERP practices with your therapist present can be a helpful stepping-stone to doing those same practices on your own. When Gina decided to resume treatment, her therapist had retired, but with the help of a new therapist, she started working on her sexual orientation obsessions again. The new therapist went with Gina to places that felt too difficult to face on her own. Gina explained, "Each time my therapist suggested an exposure, I'd tell her the same thing I'd told my first therapist, 'No way!' But this doctor didn't back off." Gina's therapist accompanied her when walking into a gay bar and went to lunch with her at a restaurant with many gay patrons. Eventually, Gina completed all of the ERP practices on her hierarchy, including some difficult items that she did on her own: calling for information about a gay pride parade, putting a gay pride sticker in her bathroom, and sitting with her best friend in her bedroom at night, with candles lit to create a romantic atmosphere.

Similarly, Ted's therapist suggested that she accompany him to the drugstore near her office while he practiced making comments about products, such as "Lead in toothpaste and children's toys isn't harmful." Ted loudly repeated these statements multiple times at the drug store. Here's how he described what he learned:

When we got back to the office, we discussed how I felt about this exposure. I said that it had been somewhat scary, but at the same time, because my therapist had designed this exposure, I was comfortable with it. Maybe it has elements of reassurance, but doing ERP with a therapist can have this effect. At my next session my therapist offered to go with me again, but the previous session had done the trick. I was able to intentionally make misstatements on my own.

Your therapist may have other ideas about how you can jump-start difficult practices. You can break down hierarchy items into smaller, more manageable steps if something feels too challenging to take on all at once. You might bring objects from home to therapy sessions to practice ERP with your therapist before returning home to practice with those same objects on your own. I'm always looking for creative ways to practice ERP with clients. For example, we might walk down the street together repeating certain words or touching feared objects. If possible, I go to clients' homes to help them begin difficult ERP practices. Of course, this is just a stepping-stone to help them do those same practices, and different practices, on their own.

Obstacle: Not Wanting to Spoil Things

If you've worked to decontaminate or make things perfect, you may find it difficult to do ERP practices that involve intentionally "spoiling" what you've worked so hard to achieve. You may have worked diligently for years to keep your home as free from contamination as possible. Your work space may be arranged in a certain way to achieve that "just right" feeling. Limited or isolated ERP practices may feel more manageable than taking actions that disrupt what you have tried so hard to protect. For example, allowing people into your home as part of an ERP practice can be especially distressing if you've spent months or years protecting your home from contamination by not allowing strangers to visit; in addition to the difficulty of the particular ERP exposure, you'd be intentionally "spoiling" the many months or even years of work you devoted to keeping your home free from contamination. Once you do it, you can't take it back. All of your previous efforts will be undone, and this prospect may create a surge of fear or dread.

Suggestions

Keep in mind that your ultimate goal is actually to spoil what you've tried to achieve through your past use of compulsions and avoidance to decrease distress. In ERP, you're learning to live with uncertainty, imperfections, not achieving "just right" feelings, and having disturbing thoughts. This means letting go of trying to control your environment so as to prevent these themes from being triggered. Take a moment to remember your greater goals. To overcome OCD, you'll need to let go of old behaviors. When this feels difficult, remember why you want to break free from the OCD cycle. Remind yourself of your values and the things in life that are more important to you than safeguarding your compulsions.

Obstacle: Confusion About Treatment Goals

At some point during treatment, almost all of my clients have come into a session and told me that they did terribly since we last met. Early on, my first thought was usually that they didn't practice leaning in, didn't refrain from using compulsions, or didn't follow through with therapy homework. Over the years, I've learned not to make these assumptions too quickly. When I ask about what went wrong, I often hear explanations such as "I was triggered by so many things this week. Triggers that had stopped bothering me made me really anxious again." When I ask about they handled those triggers, they often offer great responses about trying to lean in and not using compulsions. When I tell them that's great, they say, "But old triggers bothered me again this week and I felt really anxious. I'm backsliding. I must be doing something wrong. I thought I was finally over that particular fear."

If this obstacle sounds familiar, you may be viewing obsessions, anxiety, and urges to engage in compulsions as failures. Remember, you can't stop thoughts, urges, or images from entering your mind. Having them is not a failure. Feeling anxious is not a failure. In fact, you're actively trying to practice leaning in toward your obsessions and anxiety. And because you can't control having the *urge* to engage in a compulsion, that's not a failure either. So if you don't use a compulsion, where's the failure?

After experiencing some success in treatment, it's easy to feel discouraged when you struggle with familiar OCD triggers and fears you thought you had overcome. It's important to remember that your goal isn't to work your way through an ERP hierarchy and never think about those triggers or fears again. Familiar triggers are likely to resurface. The goal is to allow thoughts and feelings to arise and continue to change how you respond to them.

Suggestions

Remember that your goal is to respond to underlying OCD themes no matter when they're triggered or what form they take. The fact that it becomes easier to face some OCD triggers and fears doesn't mean that those triggers and fears will never bother you again. It's natural that they will, because they represent underlying OCD themes. As soon as you congratulate yourself for not being bothered by an OCD trigger, you'll probably start thinking about that trigger and obsession again. As you've learned, the more you try not to have a thought, the more it intrudes. That's the nature of thoughts—and the nature of OCD. The goal isn't to "get over" triggering obsessions; it's to change how you respond whenever and however they pop up.

As mentioned in chapter 6, it's important to keep this definition of success in mind when making entries in your positive steps log. If you start gauging success by not being triggered by obsessions or not experiencing urges to engage in compulsions, you'll be setting yourself up for disappointment. Instead, success is defined by engaging in new responses to whatever triggers, obsessions, and urges you experience. Remember to keep your eye on the right goal.

Obstacle: Interference from Other Parts of Life

A lot happens in life outside of treatment for OCD. Life goes on, and new challenges may unexpectedly arise and affect your treatment plans. Family members may come for an extended visit; they might be supportive of your treatment, or they might be critical and judgmental about your symptoms. Getting a new pet can trigger new harming fears. Pregnancy can trigger an increase in symptom severity. Starting a new job or receiving a promotion may increase your level of responsibility and trigger themes of uncertainty, excessive responsibility, or perfectionism. Moving to a new location can cause you to experience triggers you hadn't encountered before. Family events or job responsibilities may require you to travel, shake hands with new people, or sleep in hotel rooms, triggering contamination fears.

Sometimes changes in your treatment plan or in your therapist's life may feel disruptive. Gina's first therapist retired, and Ted's therapist went on extended maternity leave and referred him to someone else. Even planned changes in treatment may present obstacles. For example, if you attend intensive treatment away from home, you'll eventually move on, perhaps transitioning to regular outpatient sessions with another therapist. Transitions like these can be unsettling, especially if uncertainty triggers an onslaught of questions regarding whether a new therapist is capable of understanding your problem as well as your previous therapist did.

Suggestions

You can't control everything in life, but you can try to plan ahead when possible. You may not be able to predict that your therapist will go on leave or move to a different city, but many life events are fairly predictable. Amidst your other obligations and activities, be sure to carve out the time you need to prioritize treatment. If you anticipate major life changes, events, or stressors, plan ahead with your therapist to take them into account during treatment.

Also keep in mind that obstacles can be learning opportunities. Life events outside of treatment can create a new context in which to practice ERP and respond flexibly to spontaneous triggers. You may find that unexpected twists and turns in life allow you to make great strides in treatment.

Obstacle: Being Tempted to Stop Before Treatment Is Finished

It can be tempting to end treatment before you've met your treatment goals. People commonly encounter this obstacle after achieving enough relief from their symptoms to feel better but before facing some of their hardest ERP practices. I frequently see clients struggle with the decision to continue treatment once they hit a plateau and feel much improved. In spite of their progress, they still hope to avoid facing their greatest fears. Staggering the difficulty levels of ERP practices can help prevent you from facing this obstacle. Instead of building up to and anticipating exposures to situations that provoke the greatest distress, you face situations of varying degrees of anticipated difficulty along the way. If you delay facing your greatest fears as long as you can, your anticipatory anxiety can build. You might conclude that you've learned enough and discontinue treatment. Of course, that would only strengthen the belief that you couldn't handle facing your greatest fears or that negative outcomes would be likely.

Even though Gina successfully faced all of her harming fears, doubts about her sexual orientation only worsened until she found a new therapist and faced all of her fears. You might feel tempted to take a break from treatment, especially once you've accomplished a lot and reclaimed much of your life from the grip of OCD. But after everything you've read, you know what will happen: if you avoid facing some triggers or obsessions, and if you continue to engage in compulsions, avoidance, or reassurance seeking, you'll continue to strengthen the belief that obsessions are dangerous and that you aren't capable of tolerating the discomfort without using compulsions. This strengthens the OCD cycle and sets you up for relapse.

Similarly, it may become tempting to think something like, *I've been doing so well. I deserve a break. Giving in to a few compulsions won't hurt.* While it's true that giving in to a compulsion every once in a while won't be the end of the world, giving yourself permission to use compulsions, even when you think you deserve a break after working so hard, only sets you up for relapse. If you reward yourself by taking a free pass and not leaning in toward your fears, you're feeding into the OCD cycle once again.

Suggestions

Commit to treatment from the get-go. By making an agreement with yourself that you're willing to commit to fully engaging in treatment rather than dabbling in it or doing it halfway, you set yourself up for success. If you feel tempted to discontinue treatment prematurely, review your responses to the exercises in chapters 3 and 4 about why treatment is worth it. If you start to engage in avoidance or perhaps waver in your commitment to response prevention, think through the advantages and disadvantages of your choices or, better yet, list the advantages and disadvantages in your journal. Discuss your thoughts about discontinuing treatment with your therapist.

Most importantly, consider your future. Triggers of obsessions and urges to engage in compulsions won't just go away or disappear forever. In fact, they're likely to intensify if you start resorting to compulsions again. Completing treatment will help you successfully plan ahead for managing future OCD triggers. All of the hard work you do now will help you enjoy a future that isn't constrained by OCD.

Obstacle: Significant Others

As discussed in chapter 3, including your spouse or significant other in treatment can be instrumental in helping you achieve your goals. Loved ones can support you during difficult times, provide encouragement, and learn what to say or do when you experience obsessions and urges to engage in compulsions. Yet family members can also interfere or inadvertently impede treatment if they don't understand how it works. In particular, they may think they're being supportive and loving by offering reassurance or assisting in rituals or avoidance, not realizing that this can obstruct your efforts to use response prevention.

Family members may also become frustrated. They might feel that you don't understand or aren't supportive when they explain how your OCD affects them. Your loved ones might feel worn out by your reassurance seeking and annoyed by your rituals, and this may make it hard for them to be emotionally supportive while you're engaging in difficult ERP practices. And if they don't understand how treatment works, they may have unrealistic expectations about your treatment progress and goals.

Suggestions

If your spouse or significant other hasn't been involved in your treatment, you might ask him or her to attend a session. You might also consider asking other family members or friends to support you. Perhaps you have a parent, sibling, or good friend who wants to play a supportive role in your treatment. You can talk this through with your therapist and consider advantages and disadvantages of bringing loved ones into your treatment. Ideally, your loved ones will be supportive of your treatment plan and attend sessions whenever it's helpful. If you haven't begun treatment, you can start having discussions with them about the possibility of involving them in treatment sessions. Discuss these options when you meet with your therapist. Not all therapists work alike, and deciding whether to include family members in your treatment, and if so how to include them, is best discussed early on.

Sometimes asking loved ones to participate in your treatment may increase your anxiety, especially if they have unrealistic expectations about your symptoms or progress. They may think you should simply stop engaging in all compulsions right away, and be unable to appreciate how hard ERP is for you. It's common for therapists to play a role in educating loved ones about the nature of OCD and how treatment works. If family members or friends seem to present any obstacles to treatment, discuss this with your therapist. Together, you can devise solutions or consider adjustments to your treatment plan to address these problems.

Obstacle: Feeling Like It Never Ends

As you make progress in treatment, you're likely to notice that new situations and thoughts begin to trigger distress and urges to engage in compulsions or avoidance. Facing fears and using response prevention can feel exhausting, but your work doesn't end just because you complete an initial hierarchy of triggers and situations. Remember, your real battle is learning to respond differently to OCD themes no matter what form they take or when they're triggered.

Ted described how he came to accept ERP as an ongoing process: "I couldn't wait to start ERP. I was Pollyannaish about it. I thought I'd finally found the therapy that would cure me, and I'd become as carefree as I was when I was ten years old." Ted repeatedly listened to recordings of his most disturbing intrusive thoughts, which regarded past incidents and detailed imaginary scenarios. They described consequences he'd tried to avoid thinking about, much less say out loud. He told me, "I listened every day for ninety minutes. It was tedious, but I felt I was getting somewhere. I brought my anxiety levels way down. I showed my therapist my progress record every week. It was exciting. I was so proud of myself. I had about thirty incidents on my hierarchy, and I felt that once I worked through them, my agonizing thoughts would finally cease. It's not that cut-and-dried, though. You don't finish the original list and simply become cured. I found myself adding new items to my hierarchy. Sometimes they were variations on original items on my list and sometimes they were completely new."

Ted's experience is a realistic account of how treatment works. Experiencing OCD challenges doesn't end just because you complete an initial list of exposures. However, treatment will arm you with essential lifelong tools for facing obsessions and urges to use compulsions.

Suggestions

Discuss realistic expectations about recovery from OCD with your therapist. If you lose sight of the endgame and expect never to deal with OCD triggers again, you'll feel defeated. As long as you stay focused on the real goal of treatment—learning to practice new responses to obsessions and urges to use compulsions—you'll see your successes even when new triggers arise. This will help you find motivation to persevere over the long haul.

Keep in mind the rewards for continuing to do all of this hard work. With repeated practice, response prevention will become more familiar. When you encounter future OCD triggers, you'll know what to do. Although you may be tempted to give in to compulsions, you'll remember why it's worth it to face your fears.

EXERCISE: Anticipating Obstacles

If you've already begun treatment, you may have encountered some of the obstacles I've described in this chapter. If you haven't started treatment, you may have identified obstacles that you're likely to encounter. For example, if you see how uncertainty or perfectionism is an underlying OCD theme for you, you probably also see how it could interfere with treatment. If you safeguard certain areas to keep them "decontaminated," you might anticipate having difficulty fully embracing ERP and eventually allowing "contaminated" items into your safe zones. If you think you'll need additional support during treatment, you can start enlisting others to provide that support. You might also predict obstacles that I haven't discussed. Anticipating obstacles, whatever they may be, will help you plan how to face them, work with them, or overcome them.

Use your journal to record obstacles you think you may encounter and ideas for how you might handle them. In addition, write about obstacles that you actually encounter, whether before starting treatment or during treatment, and what helped you handle them. That way you'll have a record of which strategies are helpful to refer to in the future if you feel stuck. Come back to this topic often so you can benefit from your ongoing experience. What you learn will serve you well whenever you face obstacles in the future, including after treatment has ended.

Summary

Encountering obstacles during treatment is common. On the upside, obstacles provide opportunities to learn about difficulties that interfere with treatment progress and resolve them in ways that move you even further along in your treatment. And what you learn can also help you face future obstacles. In this chapter, I discussed some of the common obstacles my clients face, and offered suggestions about how you might manage or overcome them yourself. You might predict that you'll face some of these obstacles or encounter different problems during the course of treatment. If so, try to plan for them in advance. If unexpected difficulties arise, which they often do, remember that treatment doesn't proceed in a perfectly straight line. It's not all smooth sailing once you learn ERP and start practicing it. If you keep in mind that difficulties encountered during treatment may provide helpful learning opportunities, you'll be in a good position to learn from any bumps that you hit along the way.

In chapter 8, I'll discuss realistic expectations for recovery. Although it's not realistic to expect to never have a disturbing thought, urge, or image, you can break free from the OCD cycle of responding with compulsions and avoidance. Your long-term goal is freedom from the OCD cycle. As you complete treatment, you'll be armed with tools to maintain your gains, but you'll need to continue using these tools and practicing what you've learned in treatment.

CHAPTER 8

REALISTIC EXPECTATIONS FOR RECOVERY

In spite of its effectiveness, ERP is not a cure-all for everyone. Thoughts, urges, and images can intrude at any time. You might always be vulnerable to feeling anxiety or disgust upon exposure to certain triggers. Remember, it's not thoughts and images that are a problem; interpreting them as threatening is what gets you into trouble. Through ERP, you learn that you can have thoughts and images and ride out the discomfort they trigger. You build confidence in your ability to cope with distress without giving in to urges to use compulsions. You break the OCD cycle and reclaim your life from the grip of OCD. Still, it's not over and done with just because you meet your initial treatment goals. Recovery from OCD is an ongoing process of continuing to practice new responses when intrusive thoughts, urges, or images arise.

Temptations to use compulsions, seek reassurance, or avoid feared triggers will probably persist. Therefore, a final step in treatment is relapse prevention, which will help you handle future triggers. You'll need to stay vigilant about not feeding the OCD cycle again, even in subtle ways. Remember, OCD symptoms have a way of creeping up on you. Obsessions can morph over time. So before you finish treatment, you'll prepare to handle future triggers, distressing thoughts and images, and temptations to engage in compulsions. To prevent relapse, it's important to continue facing all of your OCD triggers by leaning in toward them. Successful treatment includes practicing response prevention regularly even after formal treatment has ended, so that response prevention becomes a way of life and OCD symptoms never get the best of you again.

The irony of recovery from OCD is that in order to regain control of your life, you need to quit trying to control thoughts, urges, and images. Recovery means choosing to live your life with acceptance of uncertainty, imperfection, feelings of responsibility and threat, and disturbing thoughts. For those with OCD, this isn't an easy task. Remember, running into difficulties after treatment ends doesn't mean you've failed. In fact, scheduling follow-up sessions after treatment concludes is common. Ongoing follow-up sessions can help you continue to manage OCD triggers and maintain your treatment progress. Joining an OCD support group can also help you stay on track. What's important is that you figure out how you can best maintain your progress or continue making progress.

Mary, Gina, and Ted all achieved great success in treatment. Their lives are markedly improved because they dared to challenge OCD. Yet they still encounter OCD triggers, practice response prevention, and, at times, struggle with difficult obsessions; and they all have strategies for facing their fears. Mary contacts her therapist from time to time for booster sessions. Gina knows that she can always contact her therapist if she needs help. Ted continues to meet with his therapist regularly, but much less frequently than when he began treatment. Mary and Ted also attend OCD support groups to maintain their progress and to help others.

Life After Treatment

You've read about how treatment works. You've thought about why treatment is worth it for you and what your life could look like if you no longer felt at the mercy of obsessions and compulsions. In earlier chapters, Mary, Gina, and Ted described their lives before treatment and shared some of their experiences during treatment. In the sections that follow, they offer a glimpse of what their lives are like now and why treatment was worth it for them.

Mary

I now can distinguish a thought from a threat. I'm not bracing myself all the time for what I might encounter. I'm open to new things and feel more confident. I sometimes worry about what will trigger me, but the anticipatory anxiety has dissipated. I could give you hundreds of examples of doing things I didn't used to do because so much more of my brainpower is freed up almost every day. Things that used to spark a serious OCD reaction just don't anymore. Thoughts and images might rise up in my mind for a millisecond, but then they fall just as fast.

I was at a hospital this week visiting a friend after surgery. Before CBT, this would have been difficult. Not only would I have reacted to the idea of germs all over the hospital, but I would have reacted to the people in the hospital. I would have reacted to seeing something gruesome, someone who was ill or weird looking, or anything that just didn't seem right. This time, instead of bracing myself as I would have in the past, I easily walked through the corridors and made my way to my friend's room. Along the way, I looked around and realized that I was fine walking through the hospital. I saw a few people on gurneys and in wheelchairs. I glanced their way appropriately, smiled, and kept on walking. I soaked in the hospital environment. I leaned in. I didn't need to take a shower or wash my hair after visiting the hospital. I went on about my day!

I no longer feel fearful if people look odd or something seems off about their personality. I may still react, but it's become a new habit to "take them in" instead of turning away. Prior to therapy, a person's appearance or attitude could condemn them to my "get off me" list. Because I work in sales, this had been difficult. If I got bad feelings from clients or colleagues, usually due to how they looked or something about their personality, I would take avoidance measures. I would e-mail instead of visit. I would pass the business to a colleague. If a friend became an OCD threat to me, like Connie did, I'd have to stop hanging out with her and lie about why. Now if an old OCD feeling about someone comes up, I look straight at it. I see it and lean in toward it. It doesn't linger, and this allows me to feel really open, rather than being plagued by the shame of not wanting to be around someone or associate with someone just because of my OCD.

Like most people with OCD, I find that the things that spike my symptoms change over time. I never know what's around the corner. But these days, since treatment, I actually turn the corner without as much fear, without bracing myself, and without the constant anxiety about what I might find by going into a public bathroom, looking too closely at a homeless man's hands, going to a new restaurant, or sitting next to someone unkempt. In fact, one of the best side effects of treatment has been a growing sense of compassion for others. Instead of being grossed out or spinning out obsessing about people who trigger me, I look at them as human beings—human just like me—who may have all kinds of OCD of their own, for all I know!

Gina

You'd think that I would have felt pure happiness when I finally overcame my OCD, but actually it was anticlimactic. When I was told that my OCD had become subclinical, I felt like crying. The news was exciting but felt weird. It was almost as if I'd lost something. My emotions were a mixture of relief, happiness, and sadness. The symptoms of my OCD were my identity for thirty-three years, and then it was gone. OCD was all I'd ever known. I used to obsess 24/7, and now I hardly obsess at all.

With that said, it was a great new beginning. For the first time, I can enjoy life without it being overshadowed by OCD. I'm a new person. I have so much time to do other things. I can get up and not have my first waking thought be *What if...?* I wake up and turn on the coffeemaker without getting caught up in obsessions or thinking about the meaning of my dreams. Remnants of ERP practices, such as gay pride stickers and gay luggage tags, are lying around the house. My kids even play with them, but seeing them no longer distresses me. I don't care who sees them. It feels good to tell my husband that I love him and find him attractive without being plagued by doubts. I hadn't been able to do that for a long time because I was always questioning whether my feelings were genuine.

I recently completed my BS degree and am pursuing a new career while raising four children. I've been able to do all of this and not have a relapse! Even if something triggers one of my worries and I have an OCD moment, I know I can handle it. I'm able to keep doing everything I need to do, accepting my thoughts all the while.

Ted

For me, recovery has been a gradual and ongoing process. When I started ERP, I thought I would work through my ERP items, and when I finished the last one, my OCD would be gone. But obsessions aren't static. There's not just one clear set of distressing events. New ones always come up. So though I feel successful in my therapy, new obsessions—and some old and persistent obsessions—can still be troublesome. The most important result of my treatment is that now I know there's an answer. I know what to do: I need to practice ERP. I can't avoid thinking about the shards of glass that might be in a grassy field, an abandoned refrigerator, or those old bad welds at the airplane factory. I wish I could block off my exaggerated concerns for a while, but I can't. I have to face them with ERP. I know that now. As stressful as immersing myself in the fear might sound, eventually it leads to immense relief.

We have a garden in the backyard between our house and where our property ends with a steep cliff overlooking a busy freeway. Originally, the back fence was about ten feet from the cliff, but when we bought the house we decided to move the fence a few feet toward the cliff and plant trees, shrubs, and flowers in the area. After fifteen years of living there, one day while I was working in the garden the thought came to me for the first time that I had caused critical danger to people by moving the fence. I would be responsible for someone stepping off the cliff to his death. Maybe several people would die. Maybe hikers would walk by at night not realizing how close they were to the edge. My fence had narrowed the pathway. The sense of danger exploded in my brain, and it was hard to face the fear. I thought it might be necessary to have the fence moved. Then I recorded an imaginal exposure about this and listened to it until I brought down the distress. I accepted the uncertainty.

Therapy has brought me to a better state of mind. I've become more flexible in my daily way of doing things, and I'm much more accepting of uncertainty.

Continuing to Use Tools Learned in Treatment

Through their hard work in therapy, Mary, Gina, and Ted have all freed themselves from the grip of OCD. They're more able to enjoy their lives and pursue valued activities. For each of them, certain skills learned during treatment were essential to their recovery and have proven invaluable in maintaining their treatment gains. They've shared their experience here in the hopes that you might experience similar benefits.

Mary

I continue to marvel at how such simple tools, such simple concepts as leaning in and not avoiding things, can relieve the anguish I experienced for so long. I still have episodes, but they're much less frequent. Part of the reason I have fewer episodes is because I'm not avoiding things. When I used to engage in avoidance, I was more likely to come across something that I was dreading. Anxiety dissipates when you're not avoiding it.

I think about CBT as my toolbox now. I leave the house with a toolbox. I wake up with a toolbox and go to bed with a toolbox. The toolbox has everything in it that I need to deal with any OCD situation. And if I happen to encounter a situation that I can't find a tool for, I can call my therapist to discuss it. Even though I've been using my CBT tools for over five years since completing therapy, I'm still so amazed by how they work. After a day or two of leaning in toward whatever spikes my OCD, it feels like a little miracle takes place. It felt like a miracle the first time I experienced relief from leaning in, and it continues to feel that way. It's something I will never take for granted.

Having a toolbox opens doors for me, socially and professionally. Now that I know I have my tools, I don't avoid as many activities, work functions, and social events. If I want to avoid going somewhere, anticipation of fear is usually the problem. Once I remember my toolbox, I can lean in toward anything I encounter and the fear dissipates. I actually get excited about using the tools now!

The disgusting floor in a restaurant kitchen that I saw last weekend still seems disgusting, but I'd hardly given it a thought until I sat down to reflect on what's changed for me since finishing treatment. When I saw it last weekend, I leaned in toward it and even ate at the restaurant, and by the day after, I'd let it go. I practiced leaning in by thinking about the dirty floor. I pictured roaches dancing across it, singing, picking up crumbs along the way, and rejoicing in the dirt. I pictured the dirt getting into my food and me eating it: *Crunch, crunch, crunch…* *Whoops! I bit into a cockroach!* The more I exposed myself to the thought of that floor, the dirt, and my disgust at it, the more its grip on my brain loosened.

Gina

Some compulsions are still habits. I find myself occasionally checking the curling iron to make sure it's unplugged or the stove to be sure it's turned off. OCD still lurks in the background. When an OCD doubt is triggered, I pull out the tools I learned in therapy. Instead of fighting the thoughts, I do my best to allow them. When I feel the urge to tap something a certain number of times to prevent tragedy, I remind myself that it's an urge to use a compulsion and I walk away. Still, OCD occasionally wins. When I'm around women, I might start to question if I'm aroused. I still feel uneasy, but I know how to accept these feelings and doubts.

Sometimes when I encounter an OCD trigger I start to reassure myself, but then I step back and get mad at myself for falling into that trap. I can recognize my worries as OCD. I can tell when I get stuck on them and feel a sense of urgency to make sure that I'm okay. I'm not saying that I'll never struggle with OCD again, but now I have the tools to deal with it when it rears its ugly head.

One time I felt scared because my symptoms lingered for a week, though they weren't as strong as in the past. I realized that it was stress catching up with me. I thought about calling my therapist but then said, *I've got this!* I used my tools.

Ted

I'm highly prone to experiencing new triggers, like the cliff at the border of our property suddenly feeling like a danger, or to suddenly having old triggers rear their ugly head and tell me that I need to go back to my religious practices or I'll go to hell. It may get to me for a while, but I know what to do: practice ERP.

A big difference for me after treatment is that I don't fall into the same kind of deep-seated anguish I used to feel. Before treatment, I didn't have an answer. I felt desperate. Now, even with all my treatment, support, and awareness, I can still see or read something that triggers a memory from the past where I feel I failed to prevent damage or harm. My distress level can still reach 95, but that doesn't seem to happen as often, and when it does, I don't feel so utterly helpless and doomed. And because I know how effective ERP can be, I go into remedial action more quickly and use ERP.

Even so, seeing something like an abandoned refrigerator can still cause extreme anguish. I feel compelled to do something about it, but I don't. I still have problems making a distinction between when there's a real problem and when there isn't. Sometimes I revert back to thinking about the airplanes at the factory. I still have doubts about mixing up the names when I performed my sister's wedding, and worry about it sometimes. I can easily slide into feelings of danger or guilt, especially at night when I want to get a calm sleep. I sometimes hate to use ERP because it causes so much anxiety, but I do it anyway, repeating scenarios in my head and accepting my fears. If I feel stuck, it helps to meet with my therapist.

Parting Words from Mary, Gina, and Ted

As the book draws to a close, I'll share some parting words from Mary, Gina, and Ted offering advice and reflections on their treatment. They hope you'll benefit from their experience whether you are about to begin treatment, are in treatment, or are working to maintain your gains after completing treatment.

Mary

Even though you may think your OCD is the rarest and worst kind, there are other people who think the same. You may feel terrified to expose yourself to something you've spent your life trying to avoid. I know because I felt like this. I can't even verbally describe some of the stuff I've feared. For my image-based obsessions, much of my exposure was done by leaning in to the thought or image. For triggers like filth and disgusting objects on the street, my actual exposures were never as bad as I thought they'd be. I'd always thought it would be awful, but that was because I'd been avoiding these things most of my life. By running to the other side of the street when I saw a homeless person or by fleeing the bathroom the minute I saw a piece of unflushed toilet paper, I was turning away, which worsened my intrusive thoughts. It was the turning *in* that freed me.

ERP may not be what you think. You get to work at your own pace as you learn to accept your thoughts and images. Working with someone who's experienced in treating OCD is important. I had a therapist who knew when to use humor and told stories that showed me he really understood what I was going through. That was essential. Remember that OCD is insidious and can creep back into your life. Use your CBT tools until they become habit. Refreshers with your therapist are important for ongoing support and to keep you moving in the right direction. I also learn a lot in support groups, and I never feel alone with my OCD.

I still have fear. Every time my fear is spiked and an episode starts, the thought goes through my head, *This one is worse than ever before. It's grosser and it won't go away.* But then I use my tools and—abracadabra!—the next day the fear is less, and the day after that it's even less, and then I forget about it. Sometimes it feels like magic.

Gina

It's tempting to think, *Now I'm fine,* but then an obsession intrudes. I still have fears of one of these OCD hiccups growing into full-blown symptoms again. Sometimes I want to avoid people who know about my OCD because seeing them feels like a reminder that something is wrong with me. Even as I contributed to this book and relived some of my OCD past, I was taken back to old emotions. I would read over what I had written and begin to cry—cry hard. It wasn't until I contributed to this book that I truly realized how painful OCD is and how much my life was robbed by it. I wish I could forget about OCD, but it doesn't work that way. Accepting obsessions is a necessary part of recovery. Now that people know about my struggle with OCD and praise my accomplishments, it can be frightening when I have unwanted thoughts and I wonder if I can handle them. At the same time, I'm sort of thankful when an obsessive thought resurfaces. It reminds me of where I've been and where I don't want to return.

Deciding to share my story hasn't always been easy. Unlike more well-known types of OCD that involve washing or checking compulsions, my thoughts are especially hard to explain. I wonder, *What will people think? How will people judge me?* I think, *What if I tell this person? Will she tell other parents? Will parents be afraid to let their children play at my house with my children?* It's easier to explain hand washing than fears of slaughtering your family. A couple of years ago, I decided to self-disclose during a presentation I gave on OCD. Although it felt frightening, my presentation was well received.

Now I'm staying anonymous as I share my story in this book, and you may wonder why. As I mentioned, my form of OCD isn't as widely discussed or understood. No one wants to talk about it because of the nature of the obsessions. At this point in my life, I'm not willing to jeopardize my reputation just because some people may not understand my OCD. However, sharing my symptoms with my family helped reduce the shame I carried for so many years. They were loving and supportive, and they didn't think any differently about me. Even so, that doesn't mean my family members truly get it or understand the depth of my suffering. How can others truly understand what it's like to be plagued by unacceptable and horrific thoughts?

Of course, my therapists understood my thoughts. I knew I was in good hands because they got it and genuinely cared. I pray one day more attention will be given to my type of OCD, that more people will be educated about it and I will be able to fully let my guard down. I do strongly encourage you to share your story with those who you can trust. There really is freedom when you no longer have to hide this demon called OCD. If you're having trouble finding a therapist, don't get discouraged; keep looking for the right help. Make sure you find someone who specializes in OCD. And once you have a good therapist, don't hold back when you describe your symptoms. I know how hard it can be to lower your guard and share what you're going through, but a good therapist will understand. Even though I found the right therapist and was relieved to know that my symptoms were OCD, I still had trouble starting ERP. It seemed like it took me forever to really do it. But eventually I learned that when you try to fight a thought, you feel worse, whereas when you decide to go with it, you get better. What motivated me was my determination to be well for my daughter. When you fully engage in ERP, it's extremely powerful. Still, even when you think you have all the tools you need to continue on your own, you may need to work with a therapist from time to time. That's okay; it's yet another tool.

As difficult as the decision was to face my worst fears in treatment, I believe that God gave me the strength to do so. Some of the exposures I had to do seemed to conflict with my faith, but I knew that God knows my heart and understands that these exposures weren't for pleasure but to get well. God wants me to live my life to the fullest. ERP is anything but pleasant, but when you learn that you can face your fears and your anxiety dissipates, it's the greatest feeling ever. The decision is yours. Live life or live OCD.

Ted

I've never really stopped therapy, but I've lessened my sessions to every other month. If I get into OCD doldrums between sessions, I tell myself that I'll discuss the dilemma with my therapist next time we meet. That thought has a way of kicking the wind out of my concerns because it reminds me that support is available.

I continue to benefit from the principles of ERP, even as I contribute to this book. When I first discussed the details of my

OCD history, it seemed very distant. It was like talking about past achievements, and it felt very pleasant. At the same time, I still have many loose ends in my psyche. I'm still plugging along and trying to lead as full a life as I can. Sometimes triggers come up, especially when I vividly bring back the day I investigated that case at the airplane factory or remember the low limb that could have injured a bicycle rider. I get a surge of anguish. Fortunately, as I continue writing and facing my fears, it doesn't last long.

I attend two OCD support groups and get a lot out of them. I've met a lot of marvelous people, including people with OCD, their family members, and dedicated group facilitators. One thing I tell people who are considering treatment or just starting treatment is to know that you can list your obsessions before facing them, and then, when you start ERP, you can begin with easier ones. I hope that helps take some of the scariness out of it. I advise getting a therapist to help you do this work, and you want to be sure you find a therapist who is well-versed in using ERP.

Concluding Comments

When I started this book, my intention was to bring treatment for OCD to life by sharing three real stories. Mary, Gina, and Ted exceeded my expectations by bravely sharing their personal experiences and describing how they successfully undertook the task of facing their fears and changing their responses. As a therapist, I've learned a lot from their descriptions of working with their therapists. I hope other therapists learn from their stories too.

Since Mary, Gina, and Ted aren't my clients, I've enjoyed the privilege of getting to know each of them outside of a therapy office. They brought great insight and humor to their storytelling, and they continue to challenge their obsessions and achieve daily victories. Sometimes their victories occurred in my presence, yet had they not told me, I wouldn't have known they were silently facing triggers. Unlike media portrayals, struggles with OCD often occur without others noticing. If you were to meet Mary, Gina, or Ted, you'd never know about their obsessions and urges to engage in compulsions. You'd never know what they've endured.

For example, Mary and I first met in a coffee shop to discuss her story and participation in this book. We introduced ourselves and ordered coffee at the counter. As we sat down at a table, Mary smiled and asked, "You have no idea what just happened, do you?" I assumed that she had just encountered an OCD trigger, but I wasn't sure what to say. Mary wasn't my client, and I didn't know details about her story yet. She explained to me that the barista who took our order had a bandage on his finger, which had spiked her anxiety. I asked if she needed some time before we started talking about the book. She gave me a big smile and said, "No. That's my point! I leaned in toward my fear right away, and I'm fine." She really was. We began our conversation as if nothing had happened.

What Mary experienced was a blip and not a full-blown OCD episode because she immediately practiced leaning in toward her fear and didn't move to compulsions or avoidance. Her response to seeing the bandaged finger exemplifies what successful recovery from OCD can look like. Breaking free from the OCD cycle is within your reach if you're willing to commit to treatment aimed at accepting the anxiety and discomfort triggered by your obsessions while refraining from using compulsions or avoidance strategies. When you think about committing to treatment for OCD, I hope you think about how Mary, Gina, and Ted describe their lives now. In sharing their stories, they've provided realistic accounts of OCD and helped illuminate the path to recovery.

I also hope that what you've read in these pages has answered many of your questions about your symptoms, the OCD cycle, and how to break free. Daring to challenge OCD by using CBT, and especially ERP, means learning to accept difficult thoughts and images rather than fighting and struggling with them. It means leaning in toward your fears and discomfort and practicing new responses instead of giving in to urges to use compulsions. To accomplish these goals, it's important to remember why you're committing to doing this work. Continue to consider why it's worth it to you. This will motivate you to get started and help you overcome obstacles along the way.

Remember, you'll work closely with a therapist and take this process step-by-step. A skilled CBT therapist with experience treating OCD can guide you through the journey and assist you along the way. Family members and friends, along with people who have been or are in treatment, can offer additional support. I hope that what you've read in this book helps you move forward and commit to treatment. I wish you success on your journey toward a life free from the grip of OCD.

RESOURCES

Books About OCD and Treatment

Abramowitz, J. S. 2009. *Getting Over OCD: A 10-Step Workbook for Taking Back Your Life.* New York: Guilford.

Baer, L. 2012. *Getting Control: Overcoming Your Obsessions and Compulsions,* 3rd ed. New York: Plume.

Bell, J. 2007. *Rewind, Replay, Repeat: A Memoir of Obsessive-Compulsive Disorder.* Center City, MN: Hazelden.

Bell, J. 2009. *When in Doubt, Make Belief: An OCD-Inspired Approach to Living with Uncertainty.* Novato, CA: New World Library.

Ciarrochi, J. W. 1995. *The Doubting Disease: Help for Scrupulosity and Religious Compulsions.* Mahwah, NJ: Paulist Press.

Foa, E. B., and R. Wilson. 2001. *Stop Obsessing! How to Overcome Your Obsessions and Compulsions.* New York: Bantam Books.

Grayson, J. 2014. *Freedom from Obsessive-Compulsive Disorder: A Personalized Recovery Program for Living with Uncertainty* (updated edition). New York: Berkley Publishing Group.

Hyman, B. M., and T. DuFrene. 2008. *Coping with OCD: Practical Strategies for Living Well with Obsessive-Compulsive Disorder.* Oakland, CA: New Harbinger.

Hyman, B. M., and C. Pedrick. 2010. *The OCD Workbook: Your Guide to Breaking Free from Obsessive-Compulsive Disorder,* 3rd ed. Oakland, CA: New Harbinger.

Landsman, K. J., K. M. Rupertus, and C. Pedrick. 2005. *Loving Someone with OCD: Help for You and Your Family.* Oakland, CA: New Harbinger.

Munford, P. R. 2004. *Overcoming Compulsive Checking: Free Your Mind from OCD.* Oakland, CA: New Harbinger.

Munford, P. R. 2005. *Overcoming Compulsive Washing: Free Your Mind from OCD.* Oakland, CA: New Harbinger.

Penzel, F. 2000. *Obsessive-Compulsive Disorders: A Complete Guide to Getting Well and Staying Well.* New York: Oxford University Press.

Purdon, C., and D. A. Clark. 2005. *Overcoming Obsessive Thoughts: How to Gain Control of Your OCD.* Oakland, CA: New Harbinger.

Tompkins, M. A. 2012. *OCD: A Guide for the Newly Diagnosed.* Oakland, CA: New Harbinger.

Books About Using an ACT Approach to Treatment

Forsyth, J. P., and G. H. Eifert. 2007. *The Mindfulness and Acceptance Workbook for Anxiety: A Guide to Breaking Free from Anxiety, Phobias, and Worry Using Acceptance and Commitment Therapy.* Oakland, CA: New Harbinger.

Hayes, S. C. 2005. *Get Out of Your Mind and Into Your Life: The New Acceptance and Commitment Therapy.* Oakland, CA: New Harbinger.

Organizations Providing Information on OCD and Treatment Providers

International OCD Foundation (IOCDF): http://www.ocfoundation.org

Anxiety and Depression Association of America (ADAA): http://www.adaa.org

Association for Behavior and Cognitive Therapies (ABCT): http://www.abct.org

REFERENCES

Abramowitz, J. 1996. "Variants of Exposure and Response Prevention in the Treatment of Obsessive-Compulsive Disorder: A Meta-Analysis." *Behavior Therapy* 27(4):583–600.

Abramowitz, J., and J. J. Arch. 2014. "Strategies for Improving Long-Term Outcomes in Cognitive Behavioral Therapy for Obsessive-Compulsive Disorder: Insights from Learning Theory." *Cognitive and Behavioral Practice* 21(1): 20–31.

Abramowitz, J. S., D. H. Baucom, S. Boeding, M. G. Wheaton, N. D. Pukay-Martin, L. E. Fabricant, C. Paprocki, and M. S. Fischer. 2013. "Treating Obsessive-Compulsive Disorder in Intimate Relationships: A Pilot Study of Couple-Based Cognitive-Behavior Therapy." *Behavior Therapy* 44(3):395–407.

American Psychiatric Association. 2013. *Diagnostic and Statistical Manual of Mental Disorders*, 5th ed. Arlington, VA: American Psychiatric Association.

Arch, J. J., and M. G. Craske. 2008. "Acceptance and Commitment Therapy and Cognitive Behavioral Therapy for Anxiety Disorders: Different Treatments, Similar Mechanisms?" *Clinical Psychology: Science and Practice* 15(4):263–279.

Bell, J. 2007. *Rewind, Replay, Repeat: A Memoir of Obsessive-Compulsive Disorder.* Center City, MN: Hazelden.

Craske, M. G., K. Kircanski, M. Zelikowsky, J. Mystkowski, N. Chowdhury, and A. Baker. 2008. "Optimizing Inhibitory Learning During Exposure Therapy." *Behaviour Research and Therapy* 46(1):5–27.

Doron, G., D. S. Derby, and O. Szepsenwol. In press. "Relationship Obsessive Compulsive Disorder (ROCD): A Conceptual Framework." *Journal of Obsessive-Compulsive and Related Disorders.*

Doron, G., D. S. Derby, O. Szepsenwol, and D. Talmor. 2012. "Tainted Love: Exploring Relationship-Centered Obsessive Compulsive Symptoms in Two Non-clinical Cohorts." *Journal of Obsessive-Compulsive and Related Disorders* 1(1):16–24.

Franklin, M. E., J. S. Abramowitz, M. J. Kozak, J. T. Levitt, and E. B. Foa. 2000. "Effectiveness of Exposure and Ritual Prevention for Obsessive-Compulsive Disorder: Randomized Compared with Nonrandomized Samples." *Journal of Consulting and Clinical Psychology* 68(4):594–602.

Hayes, S. C. 2005. *Get Out of Your Mind and Into Your Life: The New Acceptance and Commitment Therapy.* Oakland, CA: New Harbinger.

Hayes, S. C., K. D. Strosahl, and K. G. Wilson. 1999. *Acceptance and Commitment Therapy: An Experiential Approach to Behavior Change.* New York: Guilford.

Mooney, K. A., and C. A. Padesky. 2000. "Applying Client Creativity to Recurrent Problems: Constructing Possibilities and Tolerating Doubt." *Journal of Cognitive Psychotherapy* 14(2):149–161.

Obsessive Compulsive Cognitions Working Group. 2005. "Psychometric Validation of the Obsessive Beliefs Questionnaire and Interpretation of Intrusions Inventory—Part 2: Factor Analyses and Testing of a Brief Version." *Behaviour Research and Therapy* 43(11):1527–1542.

Olatunji, B. O., M. L. Davis, M. B. Powers, and J. A. Smits. 2013. "Cognitive-Behavioral Therapy for Obsessive-Compulsive Disorder: A Meta-Analysis of Treatment Outcome and Moderators." *Journal of Psychiatric Research* 47(1)33–41.

Rachman, S. 1993. "Obsessions, Responsibility and Guilt." *Behaviour Research and Therapy* 31(2):149–154.

Salkovskis, P. M. 1991. "The Importance of Behaviour in the Maintenance of Anxiety and Panic: A Cognitive Account." *Behavioural Psychotherapy* 19(1):6–19.

Tolin, D. 2009. "Alphabet Soup: ERP, CT, and ACT for OCD." *Cognitive and Behavioral Practice* 16(1): 40–48.

Wegner, D. M., D. J. Schneider, S. R. Carter, and T. L. White. 1987. "Paradoxical Effects of Thought Suppression." *Journal of Personality and Social Psychology* 53(1):5–13.

Wilhelm, S., and G. S. Steketee. 2006. *Cognitive Therapy for Obsessive-Compulsive Disorder: A Guide for Professionals.* Oakland, CA: New Harbinger.

Joan Davidson, PhD, is codirector and founding partner of the San Francisco Bay Area Center for Cognitive Therapy and assistant clinical professor in the clinical science program at the University of California, Berkeley. For over twenty years she has worked as a cognitive behavioral clinician specializing in the treatment of adults with mood and anxiety disorders. In addition, she teaches, writes, and provides clinical consultation and supervision to students and licensed professionals. Davidson is founding fellow of the Academy of Cognitive Therapy and an Academy of Cognitive Therapy Certified Trainer/Consultant. She is the coauthor of *A Transdiagnostic Road Map to Case Formulation and Treatment Planning: Practical Guidance for Clinical Decision Making* (New Harbinger, 2014), as well as *The Essential Components of Cognitive-Behavior Therapy for Depression* (American Psychological Association, 2001) and videotape series of the same name.

Foreword writer **Jeff Bell** is author of *Rewind, Replay, Repeat: A Memoir of Obsessive-Compulsive Disorder* and *When in Doubt, Make Belief: An OCD-Inspired Approach to Living with Uncertainty*. He serves as a national spokesperson for the International OCD Foundation and is founder of The Adversity 2 Advocacy Alliance. Bell lives in Benicia, CA.

FROM OUR PUBLISHER—

As the publisher at New Harbinger and a clinical psychologist since 1978, I know that emotional problems are best helped with evidence-based therapies. These are the treatments derived from scientific research (randomized controlled trials) that show what works. Whether these treatments are delivered by trained clinicians or found in a self-help book, they are designed to provide you with proven strategies to overcome your problem.

Therapies that aren't evidence-based—whether offered by clinicians or in books—are much less likely to help. In fact, therapies that aren't guided by science may not help you at all. That's why this New Harbinger book is based on scientific evidence that the treatment can relieve emotional pain.

This is important: if this book isn't enough, and you need the help of a skilled therapist, use the following resource to find a clinician trained in the evidence-based protocols appropriate for your problem. And if you need more support— a community that understands what you're going through and can show you ways to cope—a resource for that is provided below, as well.

Real help is available for the problems you have been struggling with. The skills you can learn from evidence-based therapies will change your life.

Matthew McKay, PhD
Publisher, New Harbinger Publications

If you need a therapist, the following organization can help you find a therapist trained in cognitive behavioral therapy (CBT).
The Association for Behavioral & Cognitive Therapies (ABCT) Find-a-Therapist service offers a list of therapists schooled in CBT techniques. Therapists listed are licensed professionals who have met the membership requirements of ABCT and who have chosen to appear in the directory.
Please visit www.abct.org and click on *Find a Therapist*.

For additional support for patients, family, and friends, please contact the following:
International OCD Foundation (IOCDF)
Visit www.ocfoundation.org

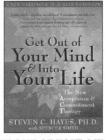